PAINTING OF THE WESTERN WORLD
POST IMPRESSIONISM

PAINTING OF THE WESTERN WORLD

POST IMPRESSIONISM

by Ian Barras Hill

Galley Press

Library of Congress Catalog Card No.
79-5365
ISBN 0-8317 7098 8
Manufactured in the Netherlands

Contents

page 6   List of color illustrations

page 7   *Chapter I*
       Introduction

page 9   *Chapter II*
       Georges Seurat, 1859-1891

page 12   *Chapter III*
       Paul Gauguin, 1848-1903

page 18   *Chapter IV*
       Vincent van Gogh, 1853-1890

page 21   Color illustrations

page 63   *Chapter V*
       Paul Cézanne, 1839-1900

page 68   *Chapter VI*
       Toulouse-Lautrec, 1864-1901

page 70   *Chapter VII*
       The Nabis, the Symbolists and the Fauves

page 72   Bibliography

Color illustrations

Pierre Bonnard   31   Nude taking a bath, c. 1937
                            32   Nude in black stockings, 1900
Georges Braque   34   Landscape at L'Estaque, 1906
Paul Cézanne   1   Young man in red vest, 1894-95
                            2   Mont Sainte Victoire, 1885-86
                            3   Bathing women, 1900-05
                            4   Still life with curtain, 1898-99
Henri Edmond Cross   19   The bay at Cavalière, 1906
André Derain   24   Self-portrait, 1904
                          25   The Thames, Waterloo Bridge and St. Paul's Cathedral in London, 1906
Kees van Dongen   27   The singer Modjesko, 1908
                          28   The Dolly Sisters, 1925
Raoul Dufy   22   The jetty at Honfleur, 1930
                          23   Black Cargo II, 1952
Paul Gauguin   13   Bonjour, Monsieur Gauguin, 1889
                        14   Jacob wrestling with the angel, 1888
                        15   When will you marry?, 1892
Vincent van Gogh   9   Four sunflowers, 1887
                        10   The sower, Arles 1889
                      11   Sunrise at Saint-Rémy, 1889
                      12   Portrait of Dr. Gachet, 1890
Henri Manguin   36   The 14th July in St. Tropez, 1905
Albert Marquet   26   Pont St. Michel, Paris, 1908
Henri Matisse   29   Still life with dishes and fruit, 1900
                      30   Lady with a hat, 1905
Hippolyte Petitjean   18   Portrait of Mme Petitjean, 1892
Henri (Le Douanier)
Rousseau   39   I myself, portrait-landscape, 1890
Theo van Rysselberghe 21   A reading, 1903-04
Georges Seurat   16   A Sunday Afternoon on the Island of La Grande Jatte, 1884-85
                      17   Model in profile, 1887
Paul Signac   20   The fort St. Jean, Marseille, 1907
Henri de Toulouse-Lautrec 5   La Goulue, 1891
                      6   The milliner, 1900
                      7   The jockey, 1899
                      8   The clowness Cha-U-Kao at the Moulin Rouge, 1895
Maurice Utrillo   38   Sacré-Cœur de Montmartre, 1934
Louis Valtat   35   Water-carriers in Arcachon, 1897
Maurice Vlaminck   37   The river, 1910
Edouard Vuillard   33   Conversation

CHAPTER I

Introduction

The decline of Impressionism - The new men - The cursed generation - "Les artistes maudits".

It is a quirk of history that words first hurled in anger by art critics at paintings they found offensive or incomprehensible have subsequently been seen to give that period of stylistic evolution its very identity. The terms "Impressionism", "Fauvism" and "Cubism" all originated this way. Ironically, these words have now slipped into the pages of history as establishment affirmation of the very abuses they sought to discourage. Dadaism, which was once thought to be cheeky mumbo jumbo, is now looked upon as a respectable movement fit for serious scholars.

The term "Post-Impressionism", although coined by the art critic Roger Fry, was not used as a derogatory classification for a younger generation's stylistic lapses. It was a convenient umbrella term for an exhibition of works by Manet, Cézanne, Gauguin, Van Gogh, Seurat, Matisse, Picasso and others, organized by Fry at the Grafton Gallery in London in the autumn of 1910. It is in fact a loose term used to denote certain trends in painting. These trends were most fully developed in the work of four men now acknowledged to be the major Post-Impressionists – Cézanne, Gauguin, Van Gogh and Toulouse-Lautrec. All four had certain aims in common. They reacted strongly against the theories of Impressionism – the need to capture the fleeting transience of life; the overriding supremacy of light; form sacrificed to sensation; the determination of the Impressionists to "banish all literary or symbolic references from their canvases". By the late 1880's Impressionist doctrines had become obsolete. This was a view held by Renoir, one of the chief members of the group, whose depiction of his favourite subjects, sensuous golden glowing bathing girls, assumed a more classical form revealing the guiding hand of Ingres and bringing back structure into composition.

To appreciate the achievements of Post-Impressionism, it is first necessary to understand the personalities of that time. All were in some way or another outcasts, refugees from comfortable middle-class backgrounds; Gauguin, Lautrec, Cézanne, Seurat all rejected their heredity. Lautrec, an aristocrat, robbed of the privileges of his class by his deformity threw himself energetically towards the other extremities of life – the brothels and cabarets of Montmartre. In Paris Gauguin was a successful stockbroker who, at the age of thirty-five, threw up his career and abandoned his wife and five children to embark on a reckless quest for artistic self fulfilment in the South Seas. Van Gogh, consumed by an ardent passion for life and art, travelled endlessly and made the greatest journey of

Plum tree, after Hiroshige, 1888
painting by Vincent van Gogh
Amsterdam, Rijksmuseum
Vincent van Gogh

L'estampe originale publiée par
Le Journal des Artistes, 1893
lithograph by Henri de Toulouse
Lautrec

them all from the cold, flat, sodden plains of northern Holland to
the fiery, sun soaked hills of Provence where the sun warmed
his loveless body but in the process burnt out his heart and his
mind. And Cézanne, the greatest solitary of them all lived in
hermit-like seclusion in Aix-en-Provence and slowly and pain-
stakingly carved out the shapes of hills and valleys, stripping the
landscape bare of all inessentials, before patiently building up
again the colours and shapes of objects in strict planes, like a
stonemason laying the foundations of a cathedral.

The points they all had in common were a) a savage commitment
to their art; b) a love of Japanese prints; c) a wish to express
a greater psychological depth in portraiture; and d) a bolder use
of shape, colour and light than the Impressionists.

What we see happening in the early 1880's is a deep questioning
principally by Seurat, Cézanne and Gauguin, of the original
premises of the Impressionist movement. All three artists had
shown at the various Impressionist group exhibitions – Gauguin
at most of them, Seurat only at the last, when his entry *La Grande
Jatte* introduced into the exhibition by his supporter Pissarro,
caused such a stir. For a long time they had adopted the high-
keyed palette of the Impressionists, and the subjects treated and
their handling of them were very similar.

CHAPTER II

Georges Seurat (1859-1891)

Neo-Impressionism - The transitional phase - The Salon des Indépendants 1884 - Paris in a ferment of new ideas in science and the arts - The Pointillist division of colours - Signac, Fénéon and "La Revue Blanche" - Seurat, a man obsessed.

Every literary or artistic movement has its leader. For the Impressionists it was Monet by his practice and example, but the prompting power behind all the Impressionist efforts was Pissarro with his eager curiosity and encouragement to new young artists. One of these young artists was Georges Seurat, a shy, reserved secretive man who, behind a placid exterior, harboured a fierce intellectuality and a seriousness of approach to his art. Seurat's distinction in the history of Impressionism was to have evolved certain theories about colour and composition which helped lead the movement out of the cul-de-sac into which it had unwittingly run. These theories were taken up and refined by disciples of Seurat − Pointillist painters such as Signac, Van Rysselberghe, Petitjean, and critics such as Félix Fénéon and Gustave Kahn. They affected the development of Gauguin, Emile Bernard and the Synthetist/Pont-Aven School and Van Gogh.

Seurat first came to the public's attention when he exhibited a huge canvas called *Bathers at Asnières* in the first Salon des Indépendants in 1884. The painting, remarkable for a young man of twenty-four had been built up from many sketches and drawings executed in the open air on the banks of the Seine at Asnières near Paris. Although fresh and light in approach, incorporating all the virtues of Impressionist technique, it had about it other qualities that presaged a move away from the accepted Impressionist formula of capturing sensations alone. There was a classic orderliness, balance and gravity about it. It resembled a fresco. Most noticeably, Seurat had used light to define his subjects rather than dilute them as the Impressionists did. The *Bathers* aroused little interest at the exhibition. Afterwards, however, the painter met Paul Signac who had admired the work, but wished that Seurat had used pure colours instead of half tints. Seurat adopted Signac's advice when he came to paint his next work *Sunday Afternoon on the Island of La Grande Jatte* and used pure unmixed colours. This was the start of the style known as Pointillism or Divisionism whose adherents maintained that ultimate colour effects could be achieved by separating out colours into complementary hues and laying them side by side with dotted or stippled touches. However, when the *Grande Jatte* was exhibited on 15 May 1886 it attracted some derisory comments, ("Call that painting? What are these stiff people,

Georges Seurat, 1883
conté crayon by Ernest Laurent
Paris, Musée National d'Art Moderne

9

The Parade, 1887-88
painting by Georges Seurat
New York, Metropolitan
Museum of Art
Stephen C. Clark collection

these wooden dolls? This cheap display of Nuremberg toys?").
Pointillism was given a nickname: confettism! In order to protect
themselves from the hostile attacks of other artists and critics, a
group calling themselves the Neo-Impressionists was formed
spearheaded by the art critic of *La Revue Blanche,* Félix Fénéon,
and the Symbolist writer Emile Verhaeren. The group included
Henri-Edmond Cross, Albert Dubois-Pillet, Charles Angrand,
Paul Signac and the Belgians Théo van Rysselberghe and
Henry Van de Velde.

Seurat was primarily a man of intellect, averse to the impulsiveness
of his predecessors the Impressionists. He dreamt of an art that
could be governed by fixed laws, and studied first the new
discoveries about the properties of colours made by the chemist
Michel Chevreul, and secondly the theories of another scientist,
Charles Henry, whose writings aided him in the development
of line and composition. He applied these theories to *The Parade,*
(1887-8) which was shown at the Salon des Indépendants where
its reception was decidedly cool. It showed a street band playing
during a carnival parade, with three bowler-hatted trumpeters and
an elegant trombonist wearing what looks like a magician's hat,
standing on a central podium. The figures are lined up like
shooting gallery targets. The critic Gustave Geffroy said of the
picture, "it has little appearance, displays a poverty of silhouette,
looks pallid and the contrasts are clumsy."

These negative comments disturbed and confused Seurat. He
decided to change his subjects and went to Normandy to paint
some landscapes and sea pieces. But he returned to his old style
with his composition *Le Chahut* which celebrates a dance routine
popular among couples at Montmartre. A critic of *Le Salut Public*
poked fun at it when it was shown at the 1890 Salon des
Indépendants. He wrote: "You would think you were confronted
with one of these coloured cartoons which act as a tapestry
pattern for porters' carpet slippers. It's enough to make you die

Paul Signac, 1889-90
drawing by Georges Seurat
Paris, Mrs Charles Cachin-Signac
collection

Le Chahut, 1890
painting by Georges Seurat
Otterlo, Rijksmuseum Kröller-Müller

laughing." One cannot help feeling that much of this criticism was made as a reaction against the obsessive seriousness with which Seurat approached all his work. Everyone knew about his painstaking methods, and admired them, but all too often the finished paintings failed to transcend those carefully prepared working sketches that form the blueprint of ideas from which he studiously proceeded. Seurat's drawings are much more imaginative and exciting. His paintings, although experimental with colour and line, can be curiously static and humourless. He was however, the first of the moderns to analyse seriously the expressive properties of colour and outline. "He wanted to know why certains combinations of tones produced an impression of sadness, others an impression of gaiety; and he had put together with this in mind a sort of catalogue in which each nuance was linked up with the emotion it suggested", so wrote Teodor de Wyzewa in an article of 1891. His fascination with the intrinsic properties of line drew him to study the figures of Greek and Egyptian statuary on urns and the frescoes of Piero della Francesca. Hence many of his people seem immobile, halted in mid-step, with their facial expressions blank, and their gazes unfocused as if in a fashion plate. What he does achieve in his vigorous glimpses of circus and dance hall life depicted in such paintings as *The Parade, Les Poseuses,* (1886-8), *Le Chahut,* (1889-90) and *The Circus* (1890-1) is a majestic calm and simple grandeur. His way of conveying movement as in *Le Chahut,* where three high-kicking performers demonstrated the current dance craze, is by a series of emphatic repetitions of image. Should the music come to life, we feel it wouldn't flow on but repeat endlessly like a needle stuck in a groove.

In 1891, Seurat showed *Le Chahut* in the Salon of Twenty in Brussels, along with four landscapes. He also sent the uncompleted *The Circus* to the eighth Salon des Indépendants. All the paintings were indifferently received. Slowly disillusion set in. He was hurt by the fact that Félix Fénéon was no longer as vocal in his support for Pointillist techniques as before. Pissarro, an early convert to the movement and the most substantial painter in the Pointillist pantheon, returned to his old Impressionist style. Its repetitive techniques had slowed down his production and inhibited his spontaneity.

Seurat died on Easter Sunday, 1891, at the early age of 32 from a sudden high fever. His work was little appreciated at the time except amongst his close followers. However, his technique had a great influence on succeeding generations – on the Fauves such as Matisse and Derain, and, in the next century, on the Futurists. He was hailed by Kandinsky as the forerunner of modern abstract painting and his reputation has always been that of a painters' painter. Because his paintings smack a little too much of theory, he has never been taken to the public's heart, like Van Gogh.

CHAPTER III

Paul Gauguin (1848-1903)

*A sailor's taste for adventure – Business success and marriage –
The bold decision to become a full-time painter and the ensuing
traumas – Brittany and Pont-Aven 1886-8 – the development of
Synthetism with Emile Bernard – with Van Gogh in Arles 1888
– in Tahiti 1891-3 – Second trip to Tahiti 1895 – Poverty, ill
health, attempted suicide – To the Marquesas Islands 1901 –
Primitivism, magic and serenity in his paintings – 1903 Death
and the Salon d'Automne retrospective exhibition.*

Gauguin was born into a literary family. His father Clovis was a
journalist and his mother Aline was the daughter of a celebrated
and eccentric woman of letters, Flora Tristan. At seventeen he
signed on as a sailor in the French navy and visited Argentina
and Scandinavia. Through his early adventures as a marine he
developed a taste for travel that was never to leave him. Returning
to Paris he joined a stockbroker's firm where he made friends
with a fellow employee, Claude Schuffenecker, who introduced
him to painting. At weekends they went out to the suburbs
around Paris to paint. In his lunch hours he walked around the
galleries near the Rue Lafitte and saw the works of Monet,
Renoir and Pissarro. At a nearby boarding house he made the
acquaintance of Mette Sophie-Gad, the daughter of a wealthy
Danish industrialist, whom he proposed to and married.

The couple took an apartment in the Place Saint Georges which
they sumptuously furnished in a manner befitting an up-and-
coming young businessman and his wife. Gauguin's business was
booming and they enjoyed a life of luxury and soon started a
family. They dressed fashionably and drove to the Stock Exchange
in a brougham. His income at that time was about 40,000 gold
francs which today would be about £9,000. They moved to a large
house with a studio in the Rue Carcel and Gauguin began to
collect Impressionist paintings, spending nearly 15,000 gold francs
on their works. He met Pissarro after the second Impressionist
exhibition in 1876 and was fired with enthusiasm by the older
man's advocacy of the Impressionist cause. He began painting
in the Impressionist manner and his work was accepted at the
fourth Impressionist exhibition of 1879 and he showed at most
of the subsequent exhibitions.

The great rage in Paris at this time was the vogue for Japanese
art. A shop selling Japanese prints and wares had opened in 1862
and soon artists came to know at first hand the works of the great
Ukiyo-e masters like Hokusai and Hiroshige and their host of
imitators. Gauguin, like Toulouse-Lautrec and later Van Gogh,
was enormously influenced by the new stark flat patterns and
bold colours to be seen in the Japanese work.

Mette Gauguin in evening dress, 1884
painting by Paul Gauguin
Oslo, Nasjonalgalleriet

Clovis
painting by Paul Gauguin
Private collection

Photograph of Paul Gauguin
probably taken in Brittany, c. 1888

Pissarro persuaded Gauguin to join him on a summer painting holiday near Pontoise and there they met Cézanne who was also working there. Gauguin already knew Cézanne's work and had bought one of his paintings. He said of the Aix master, "He's very holy for an artist... forever playing the organ." Cézanne in his turn called Gauguin "a decorator, not a painter".

What had first begun as a spare time interest now became an obsession. The stockmarket had taken a turn for the worse and there was a crisis in investment with a number of speculators and small companies going to the wall. In the face of this uncertainty, Gauguin spent more time painting at night in his studio. In 1882 he shocked his family and friends by resigning from the business to devote himself wholly to painting. Pissarro warned Gauguin: "If one is compelled to paint in order to live, one risks sacrificing one's personality to public taste."

Naturally his wife was appalled by her husband's decision. It seemed to her an act of desperate folly. They had four children and a large household with servants to support and there was another child on the way. Gauguin was now thirty-five with huge responsibilities and no visible means of support. He had thrown his lot in with the Impressionists and suffered the humiliations and abuses heaped on the group and the subsequent lack of sales. The cuts in the family budget meant they could no longer afford the affluent life style of Paris, so in January 1884 the whole family of five children and two adults moved to Rouen. Her husband's recklessness and her anxiety about the future so disturbed Mette that she decided to take the children to live with her parents in Copenhagen. Gauguin followed her there to be met with a cold and hostile reception by her parents. His apparent indifference to their daughter's fate and his foolish and selfish behaviour alienated them all. He was marked an outsider.

In order to make money he took on the agency of a tarpaulin manufacturer but failing to make sufficient sales, he returned to Paris in 1885 taking with him his favourite son, Clovis. Mette and the four other children stayed on in Denmark and she took on the bread winner's role by giving French lessons.

Gauguin took work as a billsticker for a railway company. During a bitter winter he had to nurse Clovis through a bout of smallpox but nonetheless he managed to paint and showed nineteen canvases at the eighth and final Impressionist exhibition in 1886. However, the poverty and squalor of his condition led him to leave Paris for the south coast of Brittany where he had heard that artists were well received at the inn of Marie-Jeanne Gloanec in Pont-Aven. By going there, Gauguin had decided to develop his talent in seclusion, like Cézanne. The discovery of the native Bretons in early folk costume living in a land steeped in ancient Celtic legend and peasant folk superstitions was a revelation to Gauguin. Here in 1886 he met the young painter Emile Bernard, a bright, articulate twenty-year-old who had mixed in Symbolist circles in Paris. They had many ideas and points of approach in common. Both men worked towards synthesizing in their pictures the flat patterning and simplified colours of Japanese

13

Emile Bernard and Vincent van Gogh
(seen from the back) at Asnières, 1886

art. They aimed to give their pictures a spiritual significance and transcend the mere representation of nature. They surrounded their shapes with dark lines and called this doctrine Synthetism or Cloissonism. It bore a resemblance to stained-glass art. Gauguin's restlessness took him to Martinique in 1887 in search of new themes and the year spent there gave him a taste for the bright colours and exotic subjects that found fulfilment in Tahiti years later. He returned to Pont-Aven in February 1888 and joined up with a group of painters, among them Bernard, Paul Sérusier and Meyer de Hahn who were applying synthetist techniques to their pictures. Gauguin reacted enthusiastically to this new blend of theory and subject matter. The return to the primitive sources of nature inspired him. "I love Brittany! There I find the wild and primitive. When my wooden shoes ring on this strong soil, I hear the muffled dull and mighty tone I am looking for in painting." (Noa-Noa).

Human figures now re-entered his painting as the prime focus of attention. The Impressionists, for whom visual sensation was everything, would often subordinate people to background silhouettes or unidentified shapes. The Synthetists brought back humanity into painting. Harvesters, reapers and local characters were given symbolic, even religious significance. Gauguin soon came to rely more on his visual imagination according to what was forming in his mind rather than what he saw in nature. After two disastrous months in Arles with Van Gogh in November and December 1888 Gauguin returned to Pont-Aven in April 1889 and moved in June to Le Pouldu, a fishing village a few miles up the coast. His work was beginning to be recognized and appreciated. That year he exhibited with a group called Les Vingt (The Twenty) in Brussels in February and with the Impressionist and Synthetist group in the Café Volpini in June. The paintings he did while at Arles were full of Breton references and Synthetist compositional design. His reluctance to throw off these influences became the subject of a heated debate between himself and Van Gogh and contributed towards their breach and parting. By the time he returned to Brittany he had begun to transmute the peasant folk tales of Old Brittany into religious art with a heavy admixture of self-identification as seen in his *Christ in the Garden of Olives* where his own features are those of the suffering Christ. His painting of the Yellow Christ shows Jesus nailed to the cross in an open field with Breton peasant women as weeping mourners. He later put this painting in the background of a self-portrait as if to reinforce his own delusions of victimized martyrdom.

Just as Van Gogh dreamt of bringing together a colony of artists in the South of France – Cézanne and Renoir were already there – so Gauguin imagined founding a "Studio of the Tropics" in the South Seas. Impatient now with Brittany, just as he had become impatient with Arles, he returned to Paris in February 1890 and organized a sale of his works at the Hotel Drouot a year later to raise money for such a trip. After a gaudy send-off from the Café Voltaire on 28 March 1891, he sailed to Tahiti.

14

The yellow Christ, 1889
painting by Paul Gauguin
Buffalo, Albright-Knox Art Gallery

Aita Tamari vahina Judith te Parari,
1893
painting by Paul Gauguin
Berne, Hans Hahnloser collection

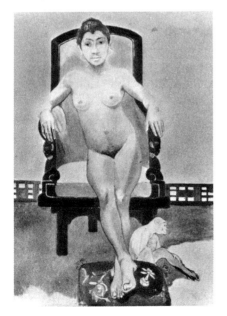

He was travelling in search of an unspoilt, native culture. Brittany had provided a genuine primordial source but was only one stage towards the primitive, innocent, absolute state of living that he knew he needed in order to rejuvenate his art. "Savagery rejuvenates me," he said, "I have moved back very far, farther than from the horses of the Parthenon, all the way back to the stammerings of my Childhood, the good old wooden hobby horse." When he first landed in Tahiti he was received in state by the French governor and the King. He stayed for a while in the capital Papeete before moving to Pacca on the west of the island, and then to Mataiea by the sea. He built his own hut and shared it with a Tahitian girl, Tehura. Impatiently he awaited the money from his agent in Paris from the sale of his paintings in Europe but it never came. He managed to eke out a scanty existence by doing wood carvings but eventually poverty and ill health forced him to leave the island in March 1893. He returned to Paris in September. Penniless on arrival, he borrowed money from his friend Paul Sérusier and in November persuaded Durand-Ruel, to hold an exhibition of his works at his gallery in the Rue Lafitte. Thirty-eight canvases from Tahiti, six from Brittany and two sculptures were put on show, but very little sold. He was by now however a legendary figure.

Undaunted and fearless, he swaggered about like a flamboyant bohemian. He painted his studio walls in the Rue Vercingetorix chrome yellow and hung his unsold Tahitian paintings on them. Dressed in a long fine cloak with mother-of-pearl buttons, sporting a grey felt hat with a sky-blue ribbon, his white gloved hand wrapped round a barbaric carving set atop his walking cane, he became a familiar figure roaming the streets of Montparnasse. At his studio he held wild parties and invited the poets and artists of the day. He lived with a Mulatto Javanese girl called Annah. In the spring of 1894, he returned to Brittany, to Pont-Aven and Le Pouldu but although surrounded by his disciples Seguin, Sérusier and Filiger, he fell into further misfortune. After a brawl with sailors at Concarneau he was laid up in hospital during which time Annah left him. He decided to leave France once and for all and by December 1894 was back in Paris to organize a sale of his work, forty-five paintings done in Tahiti and twenty-five drawings held for public sale at the Hotel Drouot on 18th February 1895. August Strindberg wrote an introduction to the catalogue. But the sale was a failure and raised only 2,986 francs. Gauguin had to buy back many of the paintings himself.

He sailed for Tahiti on 3rd July 1895 for the second and last time and went to settle in Punouavia, a village on the west coast of the island, where he found a large bamboo hut to live in. Again he waited for money to come from dealers in France who promised to sell his work. The money never arrived.

There followed a period of misery and ill-health. In 1896 the correspondence with his wife became more bitter and infrequent. He broke his foot and was constantly short of money; he had only 100 francs a day on which to support himself and his wife. In March he was plunged into despair when he learned from his

15

Whence do we come? What are we?
Where are we going?, 1897
painting by Paul Gauguin
Boston, Museum of Fine Arts

wife that his favourite daughter, Aline, just twenty had died in
Copenhagen within a week of catching pneumonia. Soon afterwards he was turned off the land he was occupying and forced
to build a new hut elsewhere. He contracted conjunctivitis, had
fainting fits, went without food for days because of lack of money
and by November 1897 was at death's door. In December, in
poverty and utter dejection, he attempted suicide. Only days
before this abortive suicide attempt he completed a massive
12 x 4½ ft. high canvas *Whence do we come? What are we? Where
are we going?,* his spiritual and metaphysical statement about the
cycle of life, a rounding off of his lifelong searches and philosophy.
In August 1898 he took an office job in Papeete in order to secure
a regular income. He had sent Ambroise Vollard several of his
pictures from Tahiti which the dealer had managed to sell but
when he returned to Punouavia he found his hut dilapidated and
many of his drawings destroyed by cockroaches.

Gauguin also came into conflict with the colonial authorities and
wrote several articles attacking the petty selfishness of the French
officials. His ill health continued but did not seem to sap his
fervour for attacking what he considered the abuses of the govern-
mental system. His cherished ideal of a perfect life in an island
paradise had taken some knocks. The dream was fast fading.

But amid these physical and moral battles some relief was
imminent. Vollard offered him a contract from France with a fixed
price per canvas. Wealthy collectors in Paris were buying his
work. But his conflict with the authorities was undermining
his will to work, robbing him of precious time.

In August 1901 he left Tahiti for a remoter island in the
Marquesas and on 16th September landed at Atuana on the island
of Hiva Oa. He bought a strip of land on which he built himself
a large hut. By this time he had lost touch almost completely
with European trends in art.

His painting had now achieved a certain serenity. After 1898 the
mysterious combination of pagan magic and religion that pervaded
his pictures had become deeper and more haunting. Again he
went into headlong confrontation with the colonial officials in
the belief that he was protecting the old pagan ways of the natives,

16

and helping them for their own good to resist the further encroachment of Western values on their fast dying culture. He urged the Marquesans to take their children away from the mission school and not pay taxes. He preached a message of uninhibited enjoyment and even called his house "The House of Enjoyment" carving its name above the door. The authorities issued a swift reprisal. He was summoned before a magistrate, fined a thousand francs and sentenced to three months in prison for defamation. By now his health had completely broken down. He was crippled from sores and abscesses and his legs were covered with eczema. He died on 8th May 1903 from a heart attack. After his death the contents of his hut were ransacked. Several erotic paintings considered pornographic were burnt by a bishop before Gauguin was buried in a Catholic cemetery. Although the South Sea Islanders were prepared to forget him, the art dealers of the civilized world were not. Vollard acquired many Gauguin works after an auction at Papeete and became chief spokesman for his art. A large retrospective exhibition was held at the Salon d'Automne in Paris in 1906 which brought together nearly 230 items and Gauguin's name was saved from oblivion as the magnificent works of his last few years were hailed as masterpieces. Gauguin's life reads like a Greek tragedy in its personal domestic complications and like a veritable odyssey in its unceasing quest for pure and primitive truths that would revitalize the sources of art. He was the first great exile, the deserter from European civilized values. In his last years in the South Seas he came to castigate those elements in bourgeois society that he saw as debilitating, bloodless and cosy, robbing art and life of its pulse and vigour. In many ways his tragedy was greater than Van Gogh's for he sacrificed more – his position in society, his wife and children and his health – for the pursuit of an unattainable ideal. His great achievement was that, ironically in the solitude of exile, he moved notions of art further forward than any man of his time. His method of covering flat surfaces with bold unmodulated colours to create an effect of overall colour harmony anticipates Matisse and Fauvism and Abstract Art. Moreover, the twentieth-century idea of the modern artist as an outcast, the man who has to destroy in order to create, "The savage Messiah", was given its first real definition by Gauguin.

Nevermore, 1897
painting by Paul Gauguin
London, Courtauld Institute Galleries

17

CHAPTER IV

Vincent van Gogh (1853-1890)

Early years – The failed missionary, teacher and art dealer 1875-82 – The befriended prostitute, Sien – The influence of Japonisme – Paris 1886-8 – To Provence "the Japan of the South" – The tragedy at Arles with Gauguin 1888 – The attack on Gauguin and the cutting off of Van Gogh's ear – Recurrent epileptic attacks and internment at Saint-Rémy 1889-90 – The brilliant, prolific last two years of his life – Suicide at Auvers-sur-Oise.

Like Gauguin, Van Gogh came to painting late in life and was largely self-taught. As with the other major Post-Impressionists, Van Gogh's development entailed journeys of self-discovery and working in conditions of wretchedness and extreme isolation. The journey was doubly intense for Van Gogh for he was a Northerner raised on the stony, cold, flat soil of Protestant Holland and he always carried with him that sense of melancholy and gloom borne of those parts. His was a passionate, mercurial nature, eager for acceptance and approval. And above all for love and trust. Denied both in life, he threw all his emotions into his art. His tragic story of personal struggle culminating in madness and suicide in 1889 is familiar to all and is kept alive by biographers anxious to reinforce the popular image of Van Gogh as the archetypal suffering Romantic artist.

The legend does little to clarify Van Gogh's art. Contrary to popular belief, he did not paint during bouts of temporary madness and not even in the "aura" that precedes epileptic attacks. He suffered from a condition called psychomotor epilepsy. The swirling rivers of paint that flow across the canvases of his Provençal orchard scenes and his last painting of crows over a cornfield are indications of how fast his style was progressing during those prolific last few months, rather than the frantic gougings of a fevered brain. At his death, Van Gogh was a full-blown Expressionist. His successors, the Fauves, all recognized it.

Van Gogh was born in Zundert, a plain rural village in northern Holland in 1853, the son of a pastor. His uncle was an art dealer who found him a job in the Goupil Gallery in London while his younger brother Theo went to work for the same firm in Brussels. Vincent was transferred to the firm's main branch in Paris in 1875 but later returned to England for a while to teach in a school. After an unhappy love affair, he turned to religion and was assigned to an evangelical mission in the Belgian mining district of Borinage. He threw himself so wholeheartedly into the cause, sacrificing both comfort and sleep, that his excess of zeal was soon regarded as religious mania and he was dismissed by the clergy in July 1879. Thwarted in his religious vocation he looked

Vincent van Gogh, 18 years old

Sorrow, 1882
drawing
Private collection

to art, and the next year started to draw miners and peasants in the style of Millet, depicting the grinding drudgery of the toil-worn labourers in the fields around the village.

His brother Theo sent him money for study and he returned to Etten, a small village near Zundert, where he continued his realistic portraiture under the tutelage of his cousin, the painter Anton Mauve. But soon Vincent was in the grip of another domestic tragedy. He fell in love with one of of his cousins, Kee Vos, a young widow with a child, who was living with his parents. At his proposal of marriage, she laughed in his face. Driven in desperation to Amsterdam, where the girl had fled to hide with her parents, Vincent begged to see her. As if to prove his love, he asked them to allow him as much time in her company as he could bear to hold his hand over a candle flame. When he acted on his words, they threw him out of the house.

One afternoon in January 1882 Vincent gave shelter to a pregnant prostitute called Sien. She became his model and companion and the two drew together in their need for love and affection. He drew her several times and one memorable drawing shows her sitting naked, hunched over with her head hidden in her arms. He was drawn to her as he was to other abject human beings with whom he came to identify, and the more so as his life went on. After he had installed her and her two children in an attic he used as a studio, he decided to move to the Drenthe province leaving her behind with the children as she refused to go with him. Drenthe was a wild marshy region and he went there to continue his peasant themes, but the people were so inhospitable that he returned to his family at Nuenen, near Eindhoven, where his father had a parish.

His influences to date had been the Old Dutch Masters and those masters of social realism Cruickshank and Doré, whose work he had seen in London. In the two years he spent at the parsonage at Nuenen he produced a vast output of work – multiple studies of hands and faces and many studies of peasant heads drawn with the passion and character of a Leonardo. His dark palette was loaded with muddy earth colours, greens, bistres and browns. The most important work of this period was *The Potato Eaters,* a sombre study of peasants sitting around a table eating their daily meal of potatoes and coffee. Vincent described the aims of the picture in one of his letters:

"I have tried to emphasize that those people eating their potatoes in the lamplight have dug the earth with those very hands they put into the dish and so it speaks of manual labour, and how they have honestly earned their food" (Letter 404).

It was a theme that obsessed him and to which he returned time and time again. He wanted the work to have the depth and message of a Rembrandt.

Vincent spent the winter of 1885 in Antwerp before joining his brother Theo in Paris where he was running an art gallery. He was to spend the next two years in the French capital, probably the happiest period of his life. He met and exchanged ideas with other artists and writers in the most fertile decade of the last

Stéphame Mallarmé with raven, 1891
etching by Paul Gauguin

1. Paul Cézanne
Young man in red vest, 1894-1895
Oil on canvas, 80 x 64.5 cm
Zurich, Collection E.G. Buhrle

Cézanne approached portraiture as
he did still life. He methodically
built up the volumes and shadows
with hatched brushstrokes and
interlapping planes. He shortened
perspective, integrating background
into foreground, focusing on the
surface and texture of painting
rather than the illusion that it aims
to represent. He had little interest
in his sitter's psychology and
would subject them to scowling
silences as he hated noises or
distraction. Ambroise Vollard, the
art dealer sat 115 times for him after
which Cézanne said that he was not
"displeased with the shirt front". In
this painting, the huge cumber-
some right arm rests on a table
top and makes a sharp angle which
contrasts with the diagonal line of
the table edge as it runs up the
right side of the picture. The
crooked left arm on which the
man rests his head, although
smaller in size, manages to
counterbalance the other, and in a
curious topsy-turvy way a real
equilibrium is achieved.

half century. Everybody seemed to be there – the Impressionists,
Seurat, Gauguin, Mallarmé, Debussy, Oscar Wilde and others.
Later, Pissarro, the patriarch of the Impressionists, recalled his first
meeting with Van Gogh, "I knew he would either go mad
or surpass us all. But I did not know he would do both."
He attended Cormon's art school. Here he met Toulouse-Lautrec,
a fellow student and a kindred spirit. Both men shared the stigma
of being denied the pleasures of conventional society. In their
art this gave them the advantage of understanding more fully the
plight of social misfits. Their portraits are perceptive, sensitive
studies of public entertainers (La Goulue) and ordinary folk
(Roulin the Postman) which record the idiosyncrasies of their
characters with sympathetic insight.

Vincent moved with Theo to an apartment on the slopes of
Montmartre and set about painting the panoramic vistas from
his window – windmills, gabled houses and vineyards. His visit
to the eighth and last Impressionist exhibition was a relevation to
him and his palette became brighter. Pissarro introduced him to
Pointillism and he visited Seurat in his studio. He also met Signac,
Charles Angrand and Emile Bernard at the paint shop of Père
Tanguy in the Rue Clauzel. He painted Tanguy's portrait against
a background of Japanese prints and quickly assimilated the
lessons to be learned from wood-block prints. In 1887 he made
copies of Japanese prints from Hiroshige – *The Bridge* and *The
Flowering Plum Garden*. Van Gogh also met Gauguin at this time
and was greatly impressed by him.

But the hectic cosmopolitan life soon tired him. Unlike Degas and
Lautrec, who thrived on artificial settings, Van Gogh yearned for
the unpretentious quietude of rural life. It was in fact at the
prompting of Lautrec that he set out for Arles in Provence on
20th February 1888 seeking not only warmth and sunlight but also
what he hoped to find in the South – "the equivalent of Japan".
The contrast in day and night-time climate was such as he had
never seen before. In the day he painted under a blazing sun; at
night the cool air descended to envelope him in mild soothing
mist. To the native Arlesians, he was a shabby eccentric who
painted on the banks of the Rhône at night in a hat crowned with
a circle of candles. He was the haloed shepherd who painted
Starry Night and the nervous, shuffling onlooker who hung
around street corners to make sketches for the *Outdoor Café at
Night*. He made friends with many of the tradespeople and
painted their portraits – the postman Roulin with his blue suit and
curly beard parted in the middle like a pair of tusks, and the café
proprietress Madame Ginoux, in traditional Arles costume.

His use of colour now took on a more symbolic, expressive
purpose signifying the violent feelings which Provence aroused in
him. He wanted "to express the love of two lovers by the marriage
of two complementary colours, their mingling and opposition, the
mysterious vibrations of kindred tone". The Neo-Impressionist
preoccupation with light had now disappeared. It was now all
colour – vibrant, ringing tones of Prussian blue, emerald green,
vermilion, and the overpowering yellow that burned from above.

2. Paul Cézanne
Mont Sainte Victoire, 1885-1886
Oil on canvas, 51.5 x 65 cm
Amsterdam, Stedelijk Museum

This mountain which looms up above Aix-en-Provence became the supreme "motif" upon which Cézanne worked out his exercises in colour and form. He painted sixty variants of it but, unlike Monet who was obsessed with the shifting play of light at different times of the day in his various series, Cézanne was more interested in how the subtle gradations of colour defined the underlying structure of the mountain. As his series progressed between 1885 and 1890, Cézanne improvised more with perspective and abandoned the conventional Renaissance rules of foreground, middle ground and background. He sought to merge the topographical features – the road, houses and arches of the viaduct into one great organic whole. By 1890 the mountain had become an object of complete intellectual abstraction with patches of the canvas left white and bare surrounded by wild splashes of colour. The townspeople of Aix hated the way Cézanne painted their landscape. They openly abused him in the street and on several occasions he was chased out of fields by farmers where he had set up his easel.

3. Paul Cézanne
Bathing women, 1900-1905
Oil on canvas, 127.2 x 196 cm
London, National Gallery.

One of the ways the Impressionists departed from the habits of the past was in their treatment of the nude for they excluded all the mythical and allegorical subjects which belonged to the classical tradition. Without these references, nakedness in painting came as a shock to a prudish age. In the paintings of the bathers that occupied him in later years and at intervals until the end of his life Cézanne had recourse to reproductions of Old Masters which he pinned on his studio walls.

In this picture he balances his leaning trees with the nudes in a symmetrical harmony in which the vibration of Impressionist blue and clarity of colour plays its part.

4. Paul Cézanne
Still life with curtain, 1898-1899
Oil on canvas, 52 x 73 cm
Leningrad, Hermitage Museum

Still life was Cézanne's major theme and, mindful of Dutch painters and Chardin, he would arrange his objects on a table with great care. His composition was always seen from a superior view. "I want to astonish Paris with an apple", he said.
An admirer, Louis de Bail, described how he watched Cézanne prepare a composition of this kind. "The cloth was draped a little over the table with instinctive taste; then Cézanne arranged the fruit; contrasting the greens against the reds, the yellows against the blues, tilting, turning, balancing the fruit as he wanted it to be, using coins of one or two sous for the purpose. He took the greatest care

over the task and many precautions; one guessed that it was a feast for the eye to him. There remained beyond the art of arrangement the sense of

the massive dignity of fold, the related rhythms and the freshness of the fruit colour against the sobriety of the cloth and the reflective quality of glass."

5. Henri de Toulouse-Lautrec
La Goulue, 1891 (Poster for the
Concert Bal in the Moulin Rouge)
Lithograph, 195 x 122 cm

This can be considered as Lautrec's
first poster commissioned by Zidler,
the director of the Moulin Rouge. In
the foreground is Valentine le
Désossé; in the centre, La Goulue. It
shows a strong stylistic affinity with
the Japanese woodcuts by Ukiyo-e
artists. Exhibited in the Salon des
Indépendants in 1892, Lautrec's
posters are masterpieces of their kind.
He had a genius for capturing the odd
and eccentric aspects of people and
places. His deft hand would swiftly
sketch in the salient features of a
subject to catch a momentary pose.
Here La Goulue is seen doing the
can-can in the background as
Valentin le Désossé moves duck-like
across the foreground. His brown
figure cuts a stark cameo out of the
light yellow of the boards and la
Goulue's dress, which in turn is set off
against the black silhouettes of the
onlookers, makes a powerful
graphic impact.

6. Henri de Toulouse-Lautrec
The milliner, 1900
Panel, 61 x 49.3 cm
Albi, Musée Toulouse-Lautrec

Lautrec's portraits are distinguished
for their delicacy of colour, brilliantly
improvised technique and, above all,
their psychological penetration. He
had a particular gift for depicting
the moods of women, whose faces in
his portraits are often tinged with
sadness or melancholy. Behind the
smile on the painted faces often lie
bitter tears. We think of the portrait of
"Jane Avril leaving the Moulin Rouge"
This is a fine portrait of Croquesi-
Margouin, the mistress of Adolphe
Albert.

7. Henri de Toulouse-Lautrec
The Jockey, 1899
Lithograph, 51.5 x 36 cm

Henri Focillon writes of Lautrec: "His
work is characterised by his highly
individual interpretation of form.
He belongs to that race of artists who
can interpret the secret poetic
language which they recognise in life's
spontaneous forms and movement.
Every detail is important in this web
of arabesques which is the start and
finish of all activity. A shoulder or
wrist caught in a sudden gesture, the
back of a hand, the wiggle of hips, the
muscles which flex and tense to
determine the unusual and yet quite
logical variations of a single pose; it is
this enigma underlying all movement
which attracts and challenges this
chosen race of artists. The real truth is
that they are infinitely more sensitive
than other men to the restless movement of living beings, and have a
special gift of mimicry which
heightens their visionary power by its
hidden watchfulness. These artists
love thoroughbred horses not for
their three-dimensional quality, but
for the elegant articulation of their
bodies seen in movement; they love
dancers, mimics, acrobats and tightro-
pe walkers, even a woman singing,
because they can watch the movement
of her throat muscles to liberate the
voice."

8. Henri de Toulouse-Lautrec
*The clowness Cha-U-Kao at the Moulin
Rouge,* 1895
Oil on canvas, 75 x 55 cm
Winterthur, Collection Oskar Reinhart

Clowness, dancer and acrobat. Her
stage name comes from the word
Chahut-Chaos (hurly-burly) used to
describe a wild dance then popular
at the Moulin Rouge. She appeared
mostly at the Nouveau Cirque and at
the Moulin Rouge.
The dancer Gabrielle is holding the
actress's arm; behind them is Tristan
Bernard in a bowler. Exhibited in
Paris in January 1896, the first owner
was King Milan of Serbia, who
paid a price then considered exorbi-
tant.

10. Vincent van Gogh
The sower, Arles 1889
Oil on canvas, 32 x 40 cm
Amsterdam, Rijksmuseum
Vincent van Gogh

Van Gogh painted this small canvas
while Gauguin was living with him
at Arles in October 1888. He followed
the lessons of Japanese art by painting
flat areas of colour intersected by
strong diagonals which isolated the
objects in the picture and by so doing
intensified them. He achieves a powerful graphic impact by imposing the
dark trunk of the tree and the
sower's body against the burning
yellow of the sun shining on the
distant landscape. The subject is an
adaptation of Millet's famous picture
and Van Gogh painted many variants
on this theme. It has a biblical
message, similar to a drawing of a
reaper done by Van Gogh. "Then I
saw this reaper – a vague figure
struggling like a devil in unbearable
heat to finish his task – then I saw
the image of Death, in the sense that
mankind itself might be the wheat
being reaped."

9. Vincent van Gogh
Four sunflowers, 1887
Oil on canvas, 60 x 100 cm
Otterlo, Rijksmuseum Kröller-Müller

These yellow flowers blossom briefly
with a fierce yellow intensity and
then die fast. Like those mushrooms
that spore at night and then dissolve
at daybreak with the approaching
light, the sunflowers bloom in the
early morning and Vincent had to rise
at dawn to catch them before they
faded. As with his famous *Sunflowers*
in a vase painted in August 1888, the
radiance of the sun, which gives these
flowers life, floods the canvas.
Van Gogh had originally thought of
doing a series of sunflowers panels to
decorate his room in the Yellow
House at Arles.

11. Vincent van Gogh
Sunrise at Saint-Rémy, 1889
Oil on canvas 71 x 80.5 cm
Nice, Private Collection

The paintings that Van Gogh made
at the end of his life when he was
living at the asylum at Saint-Rémy
have enormous force and urgency
symbolized by the swirling,
expressive lines that curl up from the
landscape into the sky. His brushwork
became sinuous and undulating to
render the effect of volumes. Like an
unending river, the pigments flow in
all directions spurting up in dizzy
spirals. The long violet strips in the
furrows punctuated by blues, purples
and reds in between are like currents
of coloured particles moving together
in one direction to converge upon a
point behind the clump of dark trees
on the left of the horizon. They
contrast with the concentric yellow
and orange rings of the huge sun on
the right.

12. Vincent van Gogh
Portrait of Dr. Gachet, 1890
Oil on canvas, 68 x 57 cm
Paris, Musée National du Louvre

Van Gogh brought to portraiture a profound analysis of character. By an expressive interplay of lines and curving arabesques with rich colours, he could suggest the moods of his sitters. "I would rather paint the eyes of men than cathedrals" he said, and he began his own extraordinary series of self-portraits. Dr. Gachet was a friend of the Impressionists, an amateur engraver and painter under whose care Van Gogh placed himself in the last year of his life. Here the intense blue of the coat contrasts with the pallor of the face. As in his own self-portraits, the restless expressive handling of the paint is the outward manifestation of the inner turmoil of the artist's own mind – the intensity of his feelings and acute sensitivity to all living things. The sensitive, resigned look of the doctor moved Van Gogh deeply. He saw in his face "the heart-broken expression of our time".

13. Paul Gauguin
Bonjour, Monsieur Gauguin, 1889
Oil on canvas, 113 x 92 cm
Prague, Národní Galerie

Gauguin was fond of introducing himself into his pictures under some other guise usually by introducing religious iconology into rural peasant scenes as if to force upon us the need to draw certain parallels between suffering biblical characters and the artist's own self-obsessed plight. He cast himself in the role of the suffering messiah in his painting *Christ in the Garden of Olives.* This image of himself is a direct reference to Courbet's famous picture *Bonjour, Monsieur Courbet* which shows the artist meeting his wealthy patron, Monsieur Alfred Bruyas on the road to Montpellier. Self-portraiture for both Gauguin and Van Gogh had a special meaning. It was their way of proclaiming to the world their independence as creative individuals. Often painted in a spirit of defiance their self-portraits are ways of recording their own ideas of themselves as they developed. It became an occupational imperative.

14. Paul Gauguin
Jacob wrestling with the angel or :
Vision after the sermon, 1888
Oil on canvas, 73 x 92 cm
Edinburgh, National Gallery of
Scotland

In 1888 Gauguin used the Old
Testament story of Jacob wrestling
with an Angel to illustrate a point he
wanted to make about how
susceptible the simple Breton peasant
women were to naive mysticism. A
group of these women are seen returning from church after having heard a
sermon on that theme and they ima-
gine they have seen a vision when
they espy two men wrestling in the
nearby fields. In the Bible story Jacob
is metaphorically wrestling with the
devil. The simplified treatment shows
the influence of Japanese print design
and the effect of the flat patterning
and rich colours, enclosed by
dark lines, recalls stained-glass
window design. The struggling figures
were based on a work by Hokusai.

15. Paul Gauguin
When will you marry ? Nafea faa ipoipo?,
1892
Oil on canvas, 105 x 77.5 cm
Basle, Kunstmuseum, Collection
Rodolphe Staechlin

This picture was painted during
Gauguin's first stay in Tahiti. He
recorded his experiences in a journal
called *Noa-Noa* (a Maori word
meaning perfume). Of the Tahitians,
he said : "These black people, these
cannibal teeth, brought the word
"savages" into my mouth... For them,
too, I was the savage. Rightly
perhaps... I began to work – notes,
sketches of all kinds. Everything in
the landscape blinded me, dazzled me.
Coming from Europe, I was constantly uncertain of some colour (and kept)
beating about the bush; yet it was so
simple to put naturally on to my
canvas a red and blue." Elsewhere in
the journal, he wrote that he wanted
to initiate himself properly into the
character of a Tahitian face, into
all the charm of a *Maori smile.*

16. Georges Seurat
A Sunday Afternoon on the Island of La Grande Jatte, 1884-85
Oil on canvas, 206 x 306 cm
Chigago, The Art Institute
Helen Birch Bartlett Memorial
Collection

Italian master Piero della Francesca. As a multi-figured composition of panoramic proportions, it is packed with information about contemporary fashion. The people are arrested in mid-step, like a single frame held in a moving film.

Seurat's early interest in the colour theories of Delacroix led him to conduct his own investigations. He did so at a time when the whole atomic structure of the chromatic spectrum was being rigorously analysed and discussed by the chemist Chevreul and other scientists. Seurat desperately wanted to understand and then control the laws of light, and feared most of all the danger of becoming a slave to its magic, as Monet and Renoir had before him. For them, light drenched and submerged all. Formlessness was reality. Seurat wanted to reintroduce classical structure, stability and permanence into his pictures. He approached his task like a scientist. He devised a method of painting with small dots of colour blue, red, yellow, orange, violet and green laid side by side, so that when seen from a distance they fused and harmonized into a whole. White, too, was used to modulate the tones. These colours vibrated beside each other to create an infinitely subtle patchwork of shifting hues and intensities. Perspectives and depth were achieved through contrasts of light and dark. Recognizing that this new exciting method of paint application pointed the way forward, Pissarro and his son Lucien eagerly espoused the cause of Seurat and his closest disciple Signac who wrote a book *"D" Eugène Delacroix aux Neo-Impressionisme* (1899) which explained the aims of the Pointillists, or Divisionists as they were sometimes called. It was through the championing of this cause that Seurat and Signac came to show their works in the eighth and last Impressionist Exhibition of 1886, where his *Sunday Afternoon on the Island of La Grande Jatte* was unveiled. As with the *Bathers* Seurat methodically built up his composition from a number of on-the-spot sketches done on the north bank of the island in a locale that became a favourite haunt of the artist. Its geometrical balance and cool pastel colouring resembles the fresco work of the

17. Georges Seurat
Model in profile, 1887
Oil on canvas, 25.5 x 16 cm
Paris, Musée du Jeu de Paume

Seurat's Pointillist method set modern
art on the road to abstraction. By
separating the application of pigment
by brush from its realistic purpose,
he asserted the paint texture in its own
right as an object of consideration
irrespective of the illusion of the scene
represented. Once the viewer steps
away from the canvas the dots fuse
and reassemble to form a recognizable
shape. This study, which has the cool
stillness of a Vermeer, was a prepara-
tory sketch for the large painting *Les
Poseuses* which is in the Barnes Founda-
tion, Merion, Pennsylvania.

18. Hippolyte Petitjean
Portrait of Mme Petitjean, 1892
Oil on canvas, 73 x 60 cm
Paris, Musée National d'Art Moderne

Petitjean was one of the many practi-
tioners of the Pointillist method who
followed Seurat's style the most
closely.

19. Henri Edmond Cross
The bay at Cavalière, 1906
Oil on canvas, 64 x 80 cm
St. Tropez, Musée de l'Annonciade

By magnifying Georges Seurat's
Pointillism, Paul Signac and
Henri-Edmond Cross pushed the
vibrating effects of complementary
colours towards pure abstraction. In
1902 Cross said : "I am returning to
the idea of chromatic harmonies
established out of nothing (so to
speak) and beyond nature as a point of
departure."

20 Paul Signac
The fort St. Jean, Marseille, 1907
Watercolour, 50 x 61 cm
St. Tropez, Musée de l'Annonciade

Signac met Seurat at the 1884 Salon des Indépendents. By this time Signac considered that Impressionism had deteriorated into a "polychrome mess" and wanted to put back some order into the use of colour. He discussed his ideas with Seurat and the two men agreed to pursue a method of painting that did away with the individualism of the single brushstroke. This would be replaced by minutely applied small dots which deliberately avoided the gestural style of a painter by its even uniformity and therefore could not distract the eye from the pure colours in the painting. Neo-Impressionism forced the eye to concentrate on the surface itself rather than the representation of outer reality. It also denied the time element so dear to the Impressionists. Seurat believed that "colour submitted to set laws can be taught, like music." Signac loved the sea, sailed in many regattas and owned thirty boats in his lifetime. In 1904, he worked with H.E. Cross and Matisse at St. Tropez and the three men opened up the dotlike technique of Seurat's into bold staccato brushstrokes which formed a patchwork of colourful arabesques on canvas. This is best seen in Signac's *The Wave* and Matisse's *Luxe, Calme et Volupté.*

21. Theo van Rysselberghe
A reading, 1903-04
Oil on canvas, 181 x 240 cm
Ghent, Museum voor Schone
Kunsten

the viewer. In 1906 Félix Fénéon
became artistic director and exhibition
organizer for the Bernheim-Jeune
gallery.

In order to protect themselves from
the hostile attacks of other artists
and critics, a group was formed
which called themselves the Neo-
Impressionists, spearheaded by the
art critic of *La Revue Blanche,* Félix
Fénéon, and the Symbolist writer
Emile Verhaeren. The group included
Henri-Edmond Cross, Albert Dubois-
Pillet, Charles Angrand and Signac.
Van Rysselberghe was a Belgian expo-
nent of the Pointillist method. In this
painting Félix Fénéon with his
goatee beard is seen leaning against
the marble mantelpiece at the back
overlooking a group of assembled
painters and literati, Octave Mirbeau
is seated in front of Fénéon, gazing at

22. Raoul Dufy
The jetty at Honfleur, 1930
Oil on canvas, 46 x 54 cm
St. Tropez, Musée de l'Annonciade

The work of Dufy is characterized by
its sparkling colour, dexterity of line
and fresh sketchlike spontaneity.
His favourite subjects are scenes of
high society at the races or on the
river. He sought out the fashionable
holiday spots and in particular the
casino towns like Deauville or Cannes
where his speedy calligraphic style
recorded the comings and going of
the "haute bourgeoisie".

23. Raoul Dufy
Black Cargo II, 1952
Oil on canvas, 77 x 97 cm
Lyon, Musée des Beaux-Arts

24. André Derain
Self portrait, 1904
Oil on canvas, 34 x 24 cm
Chambourcy, Collection
Mme Alice Derain

Derain (1880-1963) first met Matisse
at the Académie Carrière in Paris in
1898 and two years later worked with
Vlaminck at Chatou where the two
men rented a studio near the bridge,
their collaboration was the first step in
the Fauve adventure.

Derain briefly adopted the Neo-
Impressionist palette and painted
some pictures (such as *Trees* 1903) in
the Pointillist style. The next year he
painted this self-portrait which shows
the influence of Gauguin in its
application of flat areas of unmodulated colours which define the light on
the bone structure of the face. His
great wish at this stage was to bring
order and harmony to his compositions. In 1905 Derain painted two
very interesting head and shoulder
portraits of Vlaminck at Chatou and
Matisse at Collioure.

Vlaminck is shown with bright
orange hair and moustache under a
black bowler hat with the livid
expression of a bellicose colonel. The
colours reflect the violence of
Vlaminck's temperament. The Matisse
portrait shows the artist with a dark
brown beard sucking a pipe.

It is enlivened by touches of red and
ochre in the face and jacket.

Derain exhibited a number of powerful Fauve landscapes in the Salon
d'Automne in 1905 after spending
the summer painting with Matisse at
Collioure. In 1907 he gave up painting
in the Fauve manner after having "re-
discovered" Cézanne's work. This led
him towards Cubism and Picasso and
he started producing sculpture and
ceramics which he sold to Kahnweiler,
the "Cubists" dealer. He shared with
Picasso a love of African masks and
sculptures and the two men worked
together at Cadaques in Spain in 1910.
Derain's versatile talents spread into
other fields. He illustrated books and
designed stage scenery for the Ballet
Russe and other theatre companies.
After the Second World War he
settled in the South of France where
he painted realistic landscapes, still
lifes, portraits and nude studies.

25. André Derain
The Thames, Waterloo Bridge and
St. Paul's Cathedral in London, 1906
Oil on canvas, 80 x 100 cm
St. Tropez, Musée de l'Annonciade

In 1905 Derain worked with Matisse at Collioure in the South of France and his palette became lighter in response to the dazzling luminous colours he saw all around him, fiery oranges, pinks and violets. When painting the sea he would place his brushstrokes far apart and allow the white of the canvas to show through. He brought this technique to his paintings of London which he visited in 1905. He went there at the behest of the dealer Vollard in order to paint anew those Thames-side scenes that Monet had made famous only a few years before. Unlike Monet, Derain does not dissolve the city in an irridescent haze, but he does use the atmospheric flickering light of the Impressionists as seen in this picture of Waterloo Bridge. At this time colours changed to muted, colder tones of blue and green. When he returned to London the following year having seen Gauguin's pictures at Collioure in the Montfried Collection, he adopted elements of the Synthetist style. His colours are stronger and in his view of Westminster Bridge from the Thames Embankment he paints the trees pink and the river and sky yellow. He also utilized the device of curving lines to contain and harmonize the image as in his *London Bridge* painted in the spring of 1906. Further development is seen in his painting of *Hyde Park* where the distinction between the people and the trees is made by flat unmodulated tints rather than firm outline. Derain had now entered his pure Fauve stage where the brilliance of colour alone determined both light and form.

26. Albert Marquet
Pont St. Michel, Paris, 1908
Oil on canvas, 65 x 80 cm
Grenoble, Musée de Peinture et de
Sculpture.

Marquet was primarily a landscape
painter who was grouped with the
Fauves more by virtue of his subjects
than his colouring, which was sub-
dued, and his technique, which relied
on the old fashioned use of "chiaros-
curo" which the Fauves rejected. His
subjects were views of old Paris *quais,*
beaches at Fécamp, Le Havre and
St. Adresse and some fine portraits of
of soldiers and friends. He also used
black to great effect in his canvases
which was an anathema to his con-

temporaries. One of his most colourful
and popular pictures done in 1906
was *Hoardings at Trouville,* a subject
also painted by Dufy. His most fruit-
ful period was between 1904 and 1907.
Marquet always painted his landscapes
from above, leading the eye along
winding diagonal lines that recede
into the distance thus creating a deep
perspective. He was fascinated by the
humanity that enlivens a scene but he
would often reduce people to small
blobs, and only individualize them if
they showed any grotesque or excen-
tric traits. He was an exceptional
draughtsman and possessed the swift
rapier-like thrust of the cartoonist.
This is seen best in his lively brush
drawings, which range from business-

men and promenading society ladies
to cab horses and babies.

27. Kees van Dongen
The singer Modjesko, 1908
Oil on canvas, 100 x 81.3 cm
New York, Museum of Modern Art

Van Dongen kept the Fauve flame
burning at a time when the group's
enthusiasm had almost burnt itself
out. His singers and "femmes fatales"
with their dark smouldering looks and
heavy mascara'd eyes peer out at us
from garishly lit night club interiors.
Here the singer is caught under harsh
lights which accentuate the gaudy
finery and blowsy sexuality of her act.
The Russian artist Kandinsky derived
much from Van Dongen's vivid
colours and melting brushstrokes
which he carried forward to his figu-
rative canvases of 1910.

28. Kees van Dongen
The Dolly Sisters, 1925
Oil on canvas, 92 x 73 cm
Neuilly-sur-Seine, Private collection

The Dutchman Kees van Dongen first
went to Paris in 1897 having painted
city scenes in Rotterdam for several
years. He was determined to follow in
the steps of his mentor, Van Gogh.
Like his countryman, he painted street
and café scenes in Montmartre, his
favourite subjects being circus clowns,
nude women and cabaret dancers. In
order to scrape a living he took work
first as a porter at Les Halles, then as a
furniture remover and as a café portrait
artist doing thirty-minute sketches on
the terraces. For Van Dongen, life and
living were more important than art.
He had little interest in artistic theory.
"Does a man love life who spends
days patiently recording the colours
and tones of an apple?" he asked.
The women he paints are fullblooded,
sensual creatures, accomplished seduc-
tresses who are out to ensnare men.
The respectable Dolly Sisters wear
diaphanous, revealing dresses and a
suspender top peeks out from under
one leg.

29. Henri Matisse
Still life with dishes and fruit, 1900
Oil on canvas, 97 x 82 cm
Leningrad, Hermitage Museum

"I have faith that a new school of colourists will take root in the Midi," Van Gogh wrote to his brother Theo in 1888. His prayers were answered by the emergence of the Fauve group, but in particular by Matisse whose work showed the greatest creative originality and brilliance. He literally invented a range of colours which he applied from the palette rather than from directly observed nature – pinks, mauves, bluish-greens, reds and purples.

30. Henri Matisse
Lady with a hat, 1905
Oil on canvas, 81 x 60 cm
San Francisco, Collection
Walter A. Haas

The Fauves approached portraiture
with the freedom of colour they
showed in their landscapes.
Vlaminck painted Derain with a
livid red face and pipe: Derain painted
Vlaminck in the same mode with
pink face, black bowler hat, flame-red
hair and moustache. The treatment
was an outrage to conventional
portraiture. When Matisse showed
this portrait of his wife at the Salon
des Indépendents, he was booed and
his wife dared not enter. Critics believed that psychological depth had been
abandoned for colour extravagance.
The colours were deliberately
"artificial" and showed a brick-red
head of hair under a hat in which reds,
mauves, blues and greens were
juxtaposed.

31. Pierre Bonnard
Nude taking a bath, c. 1937
Oil on canvas, 93 x 146,7 cm
Private Collection

William Gaunt writes about Bonnard in the following terms: "The work of Bonnard is a delightful epilogue to the Impressionist movement, containing much of the purity of colour sensation that had been sought throughout, though he was guided by no rigidly formulated theory. Association with the Nabi group heightened his awareness of colour. He and his friend Vuillard showed the quality which earned them the title of "intimistes" depicting homely domestic interiors. Bonnard spent long periods in the south of France at St. Tropez and Le Cannet with an increase of warmth and luminosity in his colour. Like Monet and Degas, Bonnard painted a series of works with the same subject and he executed a number of informal poses of women in bathtubs. Contemplative and narcissistic, even at times wraith-like, the figures stand or recline full length in the bath. They mostly represent Marthe Bonnard, his wife, who lived what seems to have been a somewhat morbidly reclusive life in the villa at Le Cannet near Cannes which Bonnard bought in 1925. Gently floating at water surface, the figure of Marthe brings to mind the water plants to which Monet devoted the efforts of his last years. Bonnard found infinite richness in the shimmer of a limb, the colour of ripples and the golden mosaic of sunlight."

32. Pierre Bonnard
Nude in black stockings, 1900
Oil on canvas, 59 x 43 cm
England, Private Collection

Bonnard's subtle pastel tones and delicate brushstrokes are best seen in his long series of paintings which depict women at their "toilette", washing themselves or looking at their reflection in mirrors. They are casual, lingering studies far more erotic than similar ones by Degas. Through these same mirrors we glimpse the arrangement of the rest of the boudoir. Bonnard loved to group people around tables eating, and then, behind the group the eye of the viewer would be led through the French windows into gardens blooming with bougainvillea and roses, drenched by the Mediterranean sun.

33. Edouard Vuillard
Conversation
Oil on canvas, 42 x 63 cm
Private Collection

Edouard Vuillard (1868-1940) began painting with a violence of colours – flame-reds and pinks that anticipated the Fauves. He and Pierre Bonnard were the two main talents of the group known as The Nabis, formed in 1892, who, as followers of Gauguin responded enthusiastically to the new Japanese prints that had just arrived in Paris. The Nabis designed posters, programmes and stage scenery for the new Théâtre de l'Œuvre and Vuillard designed the set for Ibsen's *Rosmersholm* which was the first play put on there. Vuillard was also commissioned to decorate the drawing room of a certain Dr. Vasquez. In this wall design we see all the characteristics of his later style. A lady (presumably Mme. Vasquez) is seen playing a grand piano whilst two children look over her shoulder. In the foreground a vase of spreading flowers on a table matches the wallpaper behind. In 1896 Gauguin wrote: "Oh, you painters who demand a colour technique, study carpets!" Vuillard, in his backgrounds of flowery wallpapers, seems to have taken that advice literally! In the painting of his mother and sister of 1893 his sister seems to emerge out of the mottled brown and yellow wallpaper in her large check dress. His method of flattening his subjects into their backgrounds was aided by the introduction of electric light at the end of the nineteenth century which deepened the cold tones.

34. Georges Braque
Landscape at l'Estaque, 1906
Oil on canvas, 37 x 46.5 cm
Paris, Musée National d'Art Moderne

Braque was the son of a colour merchant and decorator and was surrounded from childhood by house-painter materials – sample boards, "grainings", "marblings", lettering and so forth. He attended art school in Le Havre. He met Dufy and Friesz in Paris, after they had exhibited in the first Fauve exhibition, organized by Matisse at Mlle. Weill's gallery in 1903 and got caught up in the excitement of Fauve colour experimentation. Braque's work was included in the Salon d'Automne exhibition of 1905.

35. Louis Valtat
Water-carriers in Arcachon, 1897
Oil on canvas, 130 x 162 cm
Geneva, Petit Palais, Musée d'Art
Moderne

As a student at the Académie Julian,
Valtat came into contact with the
Nabis and exhibited with them on
several occasions. He travelled with
Maillol to Banyuls in 1896 and
encouraged him to create his first
sculptures. Later he also took up
sculpture at the instigation of Vollard
who became his dealer in 1900. He
exhibited with the Fauves at the
famous Salon d'Automne in 1905.
Valtat was one of a group of painters
which included Henri Manguin,
Charles Camoin, Maurice Marinot and
Jean Puy who worked in the Fauve
idiom in their use of pure and vivid
colour but who brought no startling
innovations to their picture surfaces
and were content to work in a
naturalistic vein.

Like their travelling companions
Matisse and Braque, they wanted to
restore structure and solidity to
compositions but their work never
developed into abstraction. In this
picture Valtat combines the broken
flickering brushstrokes of Neo-
Impressionism with the colourful flat
patterning of Gauguin. The swaying
curvature of the women as they move
down the beach sets up a vibrant
rhythm that ripples through the
whole picture. The Art Nouveau
painters such as Klimt and Mucha
learned a lot from pictures such as
these.

36. Henri Manguin
The 14th July in St. Tropez, 1905
Oil on canvas, 61 x 50 cm
Paris, Private Collection

Manguin (1874-1949), like Valtat,
worked with pure vivid colours but
did not attempt to introduce new
daring colour combinations into his
canvases or upset the traditional
laws of perspective like Derain and
Matisse. He first met Matisse, Marquet
and Camoin as a fellow student at
Gustave Moreau's studio at the Ecole
des Beaux-Arts in 1896 and was
quickly co-opted into the Fauve group.
Although influenced by Cézanne and
Gauguin, it was the example of
Matisse's colour experimentation at
Collioure and St. Tropez that most
inspired him. It is curious though that
he never improvised more himself and
was content simply to paint bright
happy pictures of Riviera scenes that
are wholly naturalistic and break no
fresh ground. His own special gift
was an ability to incorporate the vibrating resonance of the primary Fauve
colours into a traditional landscape or
portrait format. In his portrait of his
friend Jean Puy he contrasts the
broad red surface area of Puy's
pullover with the pale delicate tones
of his face. There is nothing especially
arresting about the way he places his
sitter. Puy sits calmly gazing out at the
viewer with his right arm gently
resting across his lap.
Manguin settled at St. Tropez in the
south of France towards the end of
his life where he painted landscapes,
nudes, portraits and still-life pieces.

37. Maurice de Vlaminck
The river, 1910
Oil on canvas, 60 x 73 cm
Washington D.C., The National
Gallery of Art

For Vlaminck, painting was just like
any other physical activity such as
running, cycling or fencing. He was
no great respecter of tradition, and
rarely glanced over his shoulder, like
Matisse, to see how his painting
looked in relation to the past.
"Visiting museums bastardizes the
personality, just as hobnobbing with
priests makes you lose your faith," he
said, and the, "I have never thought
about art, classical art, Italian art, the
Greeks. I wanted to burn the Ecole
des Beaux-Arts with my cobalts and
vermilions and I wanted to interpret
my feelings with my brushes without
thinking about what had gone on
before in painting... When I get my
hands on painting materials, I don't
give a damn about other people's
painting." He believed in boldly
following his instincts and the thick
impasto textures of his paint heavily
spatulaed onto the canvas direct from
the tube reflect his turbulent and
aggressive nature.

Sacré-Cœur de Montmartre

Maurice, Utrillo, V,

38. Maurice Utrillo
Sacré-Cœur de Montmartre, 1934
Oil on canvas, 81 x 60 cm
Sao Paulo, Museu de Arte

Paris has had many interpreters but none so poignant and nostalgic as Maurice Utrillo (1883-1955). Through his melancholy, wistful eyes we glimpse the sunless empty squares and half-deserted cobbled streets that lie just beyond the busy thoroughfares of bohemian Montmartre. He shows us the other side of the village community far from the bars and cabarets of Lautrec. The buildings and streets in Utrillo's pictures are devoid of people but they seem, in an uncanny way, to reflect a deeper inner mood of the city.

Utrillo was the son of an itinerant artist named Boissy and of Suzanne Valadon, the friend and model of Renoir, Lautrec and Degas. His mother encouraged him to paint in 1902 in an attempt to wean him away from drink and for the next six years he painted street scenes and townscapes at Pierre-fitte Montmagny, a northern suburb of Paris, in a style very much influenced by Pissarro and Sisley. This is known as his "Montmagny Period". His work gradually became more melancholy in mood (as in *Porte St. Martin,* c. 1911) and he started to introduce more white into his canvases. He imitated the surface of plaster buildings by mixing white paint, glue, plaster and egg shell together, and then applying the mix onto the canvas with a palette knife. The colour combinations that he used in his first works with their red brick tones and silvery and rose greys resemble those used by Pissarro. There is a stillness and limpid calm about his churches, such as the Sacré Cœur, and his aqueducts and clusters of houses, that remind us of Corot.

Utrillo is basically an instinctive painter, a man of passionate sensibility who would paint at great speed. He used picture postcards like modern artists use photographs, to trigger off ideas for grand compositions. He had almost total visual recall and would wander about the cobbled back alleys and empty squares of Montmartre mentally recording all he saw before returning to his studio to rework his impressions into panoramic townscapes. In a painting such as *La Rue du Mont Cenis* with its row of gaslamps and peeling walls, he unerringly captures the romantic charm of Paris. His harmonies of grey, buffs, olive-greens and white are extremely subtle. Like all great artists, Utrillo preserved an innocent eye. There is a childlike spontaneity about his paintings. He seems never to have reached full maturity. However, the sense of melancholy that pervades his pictures was largely the result of his pathologically depressive nature. Painting became for him a therapeutic exercise and he was said to have painted like a man in an trance, fuelled by alcohol. In 1912, following an attack of delirium tremens, he was admitted to the asylum at Sannois and from this time on until his death in 1955 he was detained in various asylums. By 1923 his fame and reputation had grown and the main Paris galleries were clamouring for his work. In 1935 he married the widow of a Belgian banker Lucie Pauwels, and they went to live in a villa near Angoulême. Over the next twelve years his work was shown in England, the USA, Germany and Switzerland and he enjoyed a huge popularity. In 1950 a whole hall at the Venice Biennial Exhibition was given over to his work. In the year of his death he made eleven lithographs of landscapes of Paris and was at the peak of his success.

39. Henri (Le Douanier) Rousseau
I myself, portrait-landscape, 1890
Oil on canvas, 146 x 113 cm
Prague, Narodné Galerie

No account of Post-Impressionist art would be complete without mention of the one truly self-taught "naif" painter of that time, Henri "Le Douanier" Rousseau (1844-1910). He was born in Laval in 1844 into a military family and spent most of his working life in the customs service, interrupted by brief spells in the army in 1867 and 1870 during the Franco-Prussian war. In the first decade of this century he painted a famous series of jungle pictures which he claimed were inspired by the wild forest landscapes around Vera Cruz, but there is now some doubt as to whether he ever visited Mexico at all.

After leaving the army he obtained a post in the "octroi" service of Paris in December 1871. An "octroi" was a toll-house which stood at each of the city gates of Paris. Rousseau was one of the "gabelous" (i.e. minor customs officials) who levied the duty on the wine, grain, salt, milk and lamp-oil coming into the capital. When he retired from the service in December 1893 he was already quite well known as a painter having exhibited at the Salon des Indépendants for the past eight years. This painting, his famous self-portrait, was shown there in 1890. Rousseau is seen standing on one of the quays of Paris dressed in his black customs officer uniform but proudly showing off his painter status. He portrays himself very much as the accomplished master artist in full possession of his power. In his buttonhole he wears the violet badge of the *palmes académiques* (awarded to him as a teacher of drawing in a municipal school) and on his palette is inscribed the names of his first and second wives, Clemence and Josephine. The sailing ship moored near the bridge is decked out with colourful flags of many nations and behind this can be seen the newly constructed Eiffel Tower which had been erected the previous year for the International Exhibition of 1889. Everything is sharply defined in this picture, from the wine barrels beside the customs shed to the right of the picture, to the houses and chimney tops of Paris silhouetted against the sky. The air and light is crystal clear and the bold, rich use of black in Le Douanier's uniform stands out in powerful contrast to the lighter balanced tones in the rest of the picture. Henri Rousseau died on 2 September 1910 from gangrene of the leg. The following year a Memorial Exhibition was held in the Salon des Indépendants and the writer Wilhelm Uhde published a monograph on his life and work. His paintings came to be known to a wider public and his genius as the first "modern primitive" was soon acknowledged. His style foreshadowed Surrealism, and his method of introducing the illogical, conflicting components of a dream into highly realistic settings pre-dated and influenced Salvador Dali, Max Ernst and René Magritte.

He wanted to share these new discoveries with an intelligent companion. Theo sent him word that Gauguin had recently returned from Martinique. For a long time Vincent had dreamt of forming a colony of artists in the South and with Gauguin as its leader, this ideal could be realized. Theo, acting as intermediary, proposed that Gauguin should join Vincent in Arles and promised to buy all the pictures he painted there. The impoverished Gauguin, now guaranteed of an income, agreed to the plan.

He travelled to Arles on 23rd October 1888. Vincent greeted him warmly, having tidied up the Yellow House, arranged the furniture and hung his pictures up on the wall as he supposed Gauguin would like them. But right from the start there was a clash in temperaments – Gauguin was tough and proud, a mixture of expediency and generosity; Vincent, sentimental and excitable.

The two men had previously exchanged self-portraits and, prior to Gauguin's arrival, Vincent had written to him extolling the virtues of the Arlesian landscape and its women. He assured Gauguin that the colours of the South would be a revelation to him. But having already basked in the exotic splendour of the Tropics, the undulatory plains of Provence came as an anticlimax to Gauguin. At first they started to paint the same subjects – the Roman remains of Les Alyscamps, washerwomen and portraits, and a stylistic interchange took place. In the evenings they drank and talked about art but swiftly discovered that their tastes were radically different. Gauguin, classical and detached, claimed Ingres, Raphael and Degas as his mentors. Vincent admired Daumier and the Barbizon artists, Théodore Rousseau and others, whom Gauguin found crudely sentimental.

What occurred now was one of the most dramatic episodes in modern art but we only have Gauguin's account to go on – one we know to be distorted and self-justifying. The differences between the two men had reached alarming proportions.

Matters came to a head. Gauguin gave his version in *Avant et Après,* his autobiographical memoir of the events of 23rd December 1888: "I had almost made my way across the Place Victor Hugo when I heard behind me a familiar step, quick and jerky... Vincent was coming at me with an open razor in his hand. The look in my eye must have been quite stern because he stopped and bending his head, he ran back to the house."

Vincent then went up to his room, cut off part of his left ear with the razor, washed it and wrapped it up in a cloth before going to a brothel in the town to give it to one of the prostitutes he knew, saying, "Here is something to remember me by." He was found next morning in his room having lost a lot of blood and was taken to St. Paul's Hospital. On release he painted his *Self Portrait with a Cut ear.* Soon afterwards, fearing the recurrence of attacks, he committed himself to a local asylum at Saint-Rémy in Provence. As a voluntary patient he could come and go as he pleased. The former friendliness of the townspeople now gave way to fear and suspicion. He was jeered at in the street by the local children.

But none of this clouded his vision. In the last months of his life, from February 1888 to his death by suicide in July 1890 he painted

The walled garden Vincent van Gogh saw from his cell in the asylum at Saint-Rémy

two hundred pictures and did over one hundred drawings. Works such as *The Drawbridge at Arles, Harvest at La Crau, Sunflowers* and *Wheatfield with Cypresses* were all painted at Saint-Rémy. The whirling brushstrokes in the sky give a first indication of mental imbalance, but an amazing order is maintained by rhythmic patterning over the pent up violence that threatens to break the bounds of the picture frame. As with those ravishing paintings of orchards in full blossom and olive trees with gnarled trunks, all is held in check by a firm controlling hand. Common place objects – a pair of boots, an empty chair, the furniture in his bedroom – appealed to Vincent. "I am so intrigued by what really exists," he wrote "that I have neither the desire nor the courage to seek after the ideal as it might result from abstract studies."

Isolated and alone he decided to return to Paris but found that his brother had married and had just become a father. So as not to intrude, he placed himself under the care of Dr. Gachet, a friend of Pissarro at Auvers-sur-Oise, a sleepy town an hour away from Paris. There he painted the thatched cottages and wheatfields that spread across the plains, above which black carrion crows wheeled and hovered. For Vincent they were omens of death. On Sunday 27th July 1890 he walked out into the fields, taking a revolver to shoot the crows. Only days before he had written to Theo complaining of the uselessness of life. He shot himself in the chest but the bullet just missed his heart. Two days later he died. Van Gogh is one of the most popular artists of all time, a great draughtsman, whose hypersentitive temperament compelled him to depict emotional violence. He was the first Expressionist and a precursor of Fauvism.

CHAPTER V

Paul Cézanne (1839-1900)

*Middle-class background – Frustrations in Paris at trying to
become a painter – Meeting with the Impressionists at the
Café Guerbois 1863 – The violently erotic early works of his
"manière couillarde" 1863-9 – The dichotomy of his personality,
passionate sensibility v classicizing order – Scandal at the first
Impressionist exhibition 1874 – Painting with Pissarro 1873 –
Inherited wealth and marriage 1886 – The great development
period of still lifes and portraits from Paris, isolation at
Aix-en-Provence – A revolutionary landscape technique before
the Mont Sainte Victoire – Travel to Switzerland and France
1891 – Championing of his art by Ambroise Vollard 1895-8 –
Bourgeois respectability in old age – Grand Memorial Exhibition
in 1907 and hailed as "the father of modern painting".*

Paul Cézanne was born in Aix-en-Provence, the son of a wealthy
banker, and was brought up on the family country estate called
Le Jas de Bouffan, thirty-seven acres of vineyards and orchards on
the outskirts of the town. He enrolled first at the law school but
lost interest in his studies and went to Paris in 1861 with the
support of his mother to study at the Académie Suisse. Here he
paid frequent visits to the Louvre with his old schoolfriend
Emile Zola. Cézanne was wracked with misery and self-doubt
about his abilities as a painter and his depressions were not
helped by Zola's patronizing attention. The writer was eloquent,
ambitious and swept up in a welter of ideas; Cézanne on the other
hand was silent and broody and mistrusted eloquence. He was
easily provoked. Dissatisfied with a portrait of Zola that he was
working on, he first tore out the canvas in the frame then broke
up the furniture. Penniless and despondent, he returned to Aix
and took a job in his father's bank before leaving again for Paris
with an allowance. This time, he met Manet and the Impressionist
circle at the Café Guerbois, but felt ill-at-ease with their refined
talk and manners, and reacted by acting and dressing like a coarse
peasant. Manet's fastidiousness particularly irritated him and once,
when asked by the older painter what he was planning to show
at the next exhibition, he replied "a bowl of slops!"
In his own work Cézanne found inspiration for subjects from the
paintings of the Venetians in the museums and from Caravaggio,
Rubens, Goya, El Greco and Delacroix. This was known as his
"black phase", or what he referred to later on as his "manière
couillarde". He became obsessed with erotic dreams; in 1864 he
painted *The Orgy,* in 1867 *The Rape* and *The Temptation of
St. Anthony.* They were violent, distorted, sensual works which
showed obscene nudes with swollen breasts and buttocks, painted
in thick, impastoed colours plastered on with a palette knife and

Paul Cézanne

A modern Olympia, c. 1873
painting by Paul Cézanne
Paris, Musée du Jeu de Paume

heightened with swirling flashes of white. However, in some of the portraits the mood is more muted and realistic. *The Repentant Magdalen* of 1868 is pervaded by a melancholy romanticism as is the portrait of the dwarf *Achille Emperaire* (1866), a Provençal neighbour and a painter himself whose drawings of nudes influenced Cézanne. Another fine portrait of his romantic period is that of the critic *Valabrègue,* and both works show a restraint and balancing of tones that anticipate such later portraits as those of Ambroise Vollard and Victor Chocquet. The portraits and still lifes that he painted between 1865 and 1872 were objective exercises in compositional arrangement, balancing masses and densities without any attempt to convey any moral or psychological information about the subjects. The co-existence of these works with those in his frenzied "couillarde" manner show that Cézanne veered from one extreme to another.

This dichotomy in his nature makes Cézanne an interesting and complex man. He would swing from painting exuberant violent fantasies of sexual abandon like *Afternoon in Naples* to heavily encrusted sober portraits. He saw himself as a revolutionary and deliberately set out to shock the Salon who rejected his work from 1863 to 1865.

Perhaps Cézanne's greatest *"coup de bruit"* was made at the First Impressionist Exhibition held in the Boulevard des Capucines in 1874 when he submitted a painting called *A Modern Olympia,* a parody of Manet's famous "dirty nude" shown at the Salon in 1865. Cézanne's picture shows a black maid tearing away the veil which covers her mistress to reveal the lady curled up and naked on a bed. The whole event is witnessed by a seated man, elegantly dressed, who bears more than a passing resemblance to Cézanne. It was ridiculed by the critics and public alike.

It was the kindly Pissarro who took Cézanne aside in 1869 and advised him to dampen down the baroque violence of his paintings, and to concentrate more on studying nature, and observing its moods in a simpler, less strident manner.

In this same year, 1869, he met a young model, Hortense Fiquet by whom he had a son Paul, in January 1872. The family went to join Pissarro at Pontoise and then settled in Auvers-sur-Oise in 1873. Cézanne had to keep secret the news of his affair with Hortense and the birth of their child for fear his father would cut off his allowance. The rolling peace of the Auvers countryside helped soothe his passions and two paintings, *The Suicide's House* and *The House of Dr. Gachet,* marked a new stage in the development of his technique. Under Pissarro's influence he applied small dry touches of clotted pigment to the canvas to simulate a roughcast, granular texture. He banished black from his palette and his colours became lighter.

His art now started to assume its own personality. He showed sixteen pictures at the Third Impressionist Exhibition in 1877 where they were given pride of place, but that was no indication of their popularity. Most people, including Durand-Ruel, the art dealer, disliked his paintings. They seemed crude and offensive. Cézanne, for his part, considered many of the Impressionists' efforts to be superficial and finicky. Although a contemporary of theirs who exhibited at their exhibition of 1874 and 1877, he never really considered himself one of them. He was not interested in nature's fleeting transience but in its underlying structure. He learned from Pissarro that colours laid side by side would vibrate and complement each other, and he introduced into his paintings a sliding and overlapping technique of planes, like a pack of cards. This he found brought solidarity and structure to a picture.

He continued shuttling between Paris and Aix in the early 1880s until 1884 when he settled permanently at Aix. In 1886 he married Hortense and in the same year his father died, leaving him 400,000 francs, a small fortune. This set him free from financial worries for the rest of his life. He kept in touch with Bernard, Gauguin and Van Gogh and became renowned for his miserliness and hypochondria. From 1888 to the mid 1890s he spent most of his time in Paris and this was a time of great productivity for him. Such paintings as *Young Man in a Red Vest* (1894-5) (See Plate 1) *The Blue Vase* (1883-7), *Mardi Gras* (1880) and the many large bather compositions belong to this period. He changed his technique radically, organizing forms and colours so as to obtain the best harmonies in a classically restrained manner. In the portrait *Woman with a Coffee Pot* he applies his paints in thin layers, building up tones and contrasts similar to a watercolour method. But it was in his sequence of still lifes painted between 1886 and 1900 that he made his most profound exploration of the relation between surface and depth. For instance, his paintings of apples on plates affirm their existence in the context of the whole of the room in which they are placed rather than just on the wooden table that supports them. People used to think he couldn't draw, but the "gaucheries" were deliberate. Cézanne inclined his *Blue Vase* sideways or elongated the handle of a jug, or tipped up a plate or bowl so it appeared not to sit flat on the table top in order to emphasize the way we normally pick up and use such objects. In the same way he would turn the mouth of a glass towards us and distort the perspective. He invested the humblest of objects with enormous dignity.

Within a painting Cézanne invented light that was totally different from natural light. With this discovery, he finally parted company with the Impressionists. This he did in about 1885, and his sole purpose for the rest of his life was to integrate his revolutionary constructional technique of building up surfaces by planes of tone, with the inherent light of a painting. Using this technique he made the greatest progress in his experiments with landscape, most notably when he fixed his attention on the Mont Sainte Victoire, the huge mountain which looms above Aix. He painted it in oil and watercolour more than sixty times and with each new study he made its representation simpler. The traditional means of indicating depth by the convergence of straight lines was abandoned. He lowered the horizon line: horizontal and vertical planes overlap and are meshed together by a connecting glue of colours which defines the form as well as the light. By so doing

Camille Pissarro and Paul Cézanne

65

Cézanne overturned all previous notions of distance, depth and outline held sacred since the Renaissance.

Many of his letters to friends reveal how wracked with self-doubt and anxiety he was throughout his life. "I cannot express myself... I lack fulfilment... I am too old". He wrote. He turned to the freer medium of watercolour to further his improvisations.

He developed a passion for independence, and his large private income enabled him to paint and experiment according to his own ideals and not those of the public. He abandoned his portrait of Gustave Geffroy because his sitter kept speaking of Clemenceau whom Cézanne detested. When the dealer Vollard organized an exhibition in the artist's honour at his gallery in December 1895, Cézanne sent him his canvases rolled up without stretchers.

He contracted diabetes in 1891 which compelled him to make trips to find health cures in Switzerland, Vichy and later to Talloires where he painted the Lake of Annecy in the Haute Savoie. In this painting his method of indicating the ambiguities of depth by overlapping and receding planes is carried to its limit. "To paint a landscape well I must first discover the geological foundations", he said. When his mother died in 1897 he inherited Le Jas de Bouffan but could not bear to live there because of all the memories associated with it so he took lodgings in Aix. In 1902 he built a house and studio on the hill overlooking the town. When he went out to paint he dressed like a farmer and would ride to the chosen spot of the day in a horse drawn carriage upholstered in red velvet. This paradox was typical of his highly contradictory nature. He channelled his passions into paint and would rein in his wilder instincts, out of a a sense of propriety. Unlike his idol, Delacroix, he never combined his sessions of painting with love. In fact, in middle age he couldn't bring himself to paint women in the nude, and this explains why many of the figures in his bathing compositions are often wooden and unlifelike, painted from memory rather than first hand.

Recognition came when he was invited to exhibit at the Salon des Indépendents of 1899 and 1901 and an admirer of his, Maurice Denis, painted *Homage à Cézanne* which was shown in Brussels in 1901. Prior to this there were retrospective exhibitions held in 1895 and 1898 at Vollard's gallery where many of the younger painters saw his work. It was Denis who invited him to show at the Salon d'Automne of 1904 and the "Cézanne Exhibition" as it was called was an overwhelming success and a revelation to both artists and the public who had forgotten the painter, believing him dead. When in society he would dress up as the eminently respectable bourgeois citizen, dutifully attend mass and voice strong reactionary political views in public. Like Manet he hankered after establishment recognition. This he eventually received in 1907 when Vollard organized the Cézanne Memorial Exhibition. Forty-eight of his paintings were shown and his watercolours could be seen at the Bernheim Jeune Gallery. Some letters of his were also published that year.

Back in Aix he would go out every day and paint in the vicinity around the Mont Sainte Victoire. He spent an inordinate length

Cézanne's villa, Le Jas de Bouffan

Homage à Cézanne, 1900
painting by Maurice Denis
Paris, Musée National d'Art Moderne

of time on each canvas, returning to the subject time and time
again. He used to carry his equipment on his back and walk to
the place or "motif" as he called the day's chosen subject.

One day while trudging back home he was caught in a thunder-
storm and collapsed by the side of the road. A passing laundry
cart picked him up but he caught pneumonia and died a week
later at the age of sixty-seven in 1906.

Cézanne wanted to be considered a classical painter, "to do
Poussin again after nature". His declared ambition was to make
something solid and durable out of Impressionism like the art of
the museums. He modelled all his subjects like rocks and building
blocks, juxtaposing colour tones to suggest light changes rather
than deliberately painting in shadows. He wished to "marry the
curves of women to the shoulders of hills" and wrote "when
colour is at its richest, the form is most complete."

Cézanne had more influence on succeeding generations of artists
than any man of his time. He is rightfully referred to as "the father
of modern painting". The Cubists' method of dislocating planes
to render depth was a literal working out of Cézanne's remark
about seeing in nature "the cylinder, the sphere and the cone".
Secondly, painters like Mondrian and Malevich who followed the
Cubists' experiments through to complete abstraction are
indebted to Cézanne. The painter Robert Delauney took as his
jumping off point Cézanne's remark, "the edges of an object
vanish towards a point on the observer's horizon", and Delauney's
interlocking wheel paintings are an attempt to convey depth by
colour alone – a practice that the Fauve painters so ardently
followed. Every important artist of this century derived inspiration
from Cézanne.

"I am too old, and I came too soon, but I mark the way and
others will follow", he said to Joachim Gasquet in a moment of
precognition. His place among the greatest of artists in the history
of painting is assured.

CHAPTER VI

Toulouse-Lautrec (1864-1901)

Aristocratic background - Crippled childhood - The influence of Degas and Japanese art - The dazzling chronicler of "La Belle Époque", the Moulin Rouge of the cabaret dancers, Yvette Guilbert, Jane Avril and others in the naughty nineties - Female comradeship and strange alliances in brothels - The compassionate portraitist - The frequenter of fashionable salons - Alcoholism and paralysis - The draughtsman of genius and precursor of Art Nouveau.

Lautrec was born in 1864, the son of a nobleman, the Count of Toulouse. He was brought up on the family estate near Albi and at an early age revealed a precocious talent for drawing. A delicate child, he broke both his legs after two falls in 1878 and 1879 which retarded his growth and crippled him for the rest of his life. In 1882 he studied at the studios of Leon Bonnat and Fernand Cormon and there met Emile Bernard and Van Gogh. He also met many of the Impressionists at this time and particulary admired the work of Degas whose powers of draughtsmanship and choice of subjects – actresses, clowns, dancers, circus scenes, brothels and race tracks appealed to Lautrec. The influence of Degas is seen in his painting *At the Moulin Rouge* of 1890 and his subsequent poster celebrates the growing popularity of this music hall. It was also his introduction to a medium which he virtually made his own – lithography. He adapted the lessons of Degas and the new Japanese art to his bold poster designs which made their maximum graphic impact by striking contrasts of colour. Aristide Bruant's red scarf, casually thrown over his shoulder, is set off against his black cape and cloak which stands out from a white background.

Like Degas, Lautrec was fond of rambling from club to club, often accompanied by his cousin, Dr. Gabriel Tapié de Céleyran. He would take up his position with a sketch pad at a side table and draw with great rapidity and assurance. He loved to capture the mannerisms and projections of performers like Yvette Guilbert, May Belfort and La Goulue as they went through their paces.

The personality of a singer could be summed up in the swoop of an arm, a flick of the hips or a simple item of clothing such as Yvette Guilbert's shoulder-length gloves.

Portraits of his mother done in the 1880s show the influence of Manet and Morisot and he went through a brief Pointillist phase. His nightly forays into the gaudy world of the night clubs sharpened his colour schemes and gave him greater freedom to exercise his savage linear gifts. For ever in search of new subjects, he discovered a wealth of human vice and activity behind the dim

Toulouse-Lautrec and a friend
Paris, Bibliothèque Nationale

La Goulue doing the can-can

The Englishman in the
Moulin Rouge, 1892
lithograph by Henri de Toulouse-
Lautrec

gas-lit shutters of the city's licensed brothels. In 1894 he established himself in a brothel in the rue des Moulins and drew the prostitutes in a series of lithographs called *Elles*. He was particularly interested in the lesbian relationships struck up between the women, who clung to each other seeking a more enduring form of love. He said of the women in such places, "they are alive... they stretch themselves on divans like animals... they're so lacking in pretension, you know." His treatment of these inmates was compassionate and understanding, unlike the cold voyeurism of Degas's approach to similar subjects. Lautrec gives us an intimate glimpse of the snatched mésalliance and warm trustfulness of the women among themselves, without sentimental innuendo or moral reproof.

By 1892 he had made his reputation with his brilliant poster designs and cartoons for such papers as *Le Figaro* and *La Revue Blanche*. The doors of some of the most fashionable salons in Paris were thrown open to him. At soirées held at the house of the beautiful Misia Natanson, the young Polish wife of Thadée Natanson, editor of the symbolist periodical *La Revue Blanche* he met Mallarmé, Valery, Debussy, Félix Fénéon, Vuillard, Bonnard and Colette and he would often go to stay with Misia at her country house.

His own personal life was marred by his dwarfish size but this did not prevent him from making relationships with women who viewed him in a spirit of curious amusement combined with real affection. One such woman was his model, Suzanne Valadon, with whom he enjoyed a sporadic, quarrelsome affair. Most of his attachments though were with the prostitutes and *chanteuses* whom he frequently painted. A man of enormous energy, he needed very little sleep and was reputed to have had a voracious appetite for food, drink and sex. He became an alcoholic in the 1890s and by the end of the decade his art had begun to suffer. After an attack of delirium tremens in February 1899, he was admitted to a clinic near Neuilly to dry out. Upon release he started on his series of circus scenes and made trips throughout the year to Bordeaux, Le Havre, and the family castle at Malromé from Paris. In August 1901 he was struck down by a paralytic stroke caused by the joint ravages of alcohol and syphilis and died three weeks later with his mother at his side.

Lautrec was a dazzlingly gifted artist. He virtually invented the matrix of modern advertising art by his pioneering mastery of stone lithography. And the paradox is that by so doing he, an aristocrat, democratized art. He inspired many modern painters including Edvard Munch who saw Lautrec's Moulin Rouge posters in the streets of Paris when he was a student there in 1885, and it is to these that his *Dance of Life* is indebted. Picasso's first paintings in Paris in 1900 reveal stylistic borrowings from Lautrec.

By assimilating the curving arabesques of Japanese art and the decorative symbolism of Gauguin, Lautrec set the style for Art Nouveau.

69

CHAPTER VII

The Nabis, the Symbolists and the Fauves

Dreamwoven landscapes – Spectral shapes and the emergence of subconscious fantasies in art – Gustave Moreau and Odilon Redon – Paul Sérusier and Symbolism – Dramatic stage designs – The Académie Julian – Vlaminck and muscular painting – Burning bright colours – Matisse, Cross and Signac at St. Tropez 1904 – The Salon d'Automne 1905 – "The wild beasts" – Casino royale: Raoul Dufy and society at play – The linear decorations of Matisse and the influence of Eastern Art – Van Dongen and the demi-monde – Georges Rouault: circus, war and religious themes – Braque, Picasso and the advent of Cubism.

The monster looked at everything with horror, 1886
lithograph by Odilon Redon
New York, Museum of Modern Art
Mrs John D. Rockefeller Jr. Purchase Fund

In the 1890's Post-Impressionist art branches out in two directions. The Fauve painters took up the exuberant colouring of Van Gogh while Maurice Denis, Paul Sérusier, Paul Ranson, Pierre Bonnard and Edouard Vuillard, all students at the Académie Julian, formed themselves into a group called the Nabis (after a Hebrew word meaning "prophet" or "divinely inspired") which was influenced by the symbolic patterning of Gauguin in his Brittany days. They exchanged ideas, chiefly through Sérusier, with such dreamlike painters as Odilon Redon and the Symbolists. The latter produced set designs for the Théâtre de l'Œuvre founded in 1893 by the great stage impresario, Lugné Poe, who produced Wilde's *Salomé,* Ibsen's *Peer Gynt* and Alfred Jarry's *Ubu Roi.* The Rose-Croix mystic painters headed by Peladon charted the inner landscapes of the mind and used spectral images to bring to the surface deep-buried neuroses. Their fantasies prefigured the work of Chirico and the Surrealists in the twentieth century.

In 1901 at an exhibition of Van Gogh paintings held at the Bernheim-Jeune Gallery, a huge bluff man called Maurice de Vlaminck exploded with joy at the spontaneity and bright colours he saw in the pictures before him. The fire and vigour of these canvases ignited his senses. "That day", he said later, "I loved Van Gogh more than my own father".

Six years earlier in 1895 Vlaminck had started to paint his first pictures in his home town of Chatou. He fitted this in between cycle-racing and violin-playing in cafés. He had just left the army and was only twenty-three. In this same year, while out painting landscapes he made friends with André Derain, another artist/athlete, aged nineteen, who had studied in Paris and met Henri Matisse. Derain introduced Vlaminck to Matisse at the Van Gogh retrospective exhibition in 1901 and invited the older man to come to Chatou to see their paintings. Matisse had

Self portrait
drawing by Maurice de Vlaminck

Self portrait, 1914
drawing by Henri Manguin

previously met Albert Marquet another future member of the Fauves in 1898 at Gustave Moreau's studio. Raoul Dufy, Othon Friesz and Georges Braque were all natives of Le Havre and studied, at the École des Beaux-Arts. These artists were all soon to be known as the "Fauves". Matisse became the figurehead of the group and organized the first "Fauve" exhibition at Mlle Weill's in 1903. The other artists invited to exhibit were Jean Puy, Louis Valtat, Charles Camoin, Henri Manguin, Georges Rouault and the Dutchman, Kees van Dongen. Matisse acted as the bridgehead between Pointillism and Fauvism. He worked with Cross and Signac in St. Tropez in 1904 and joined Derain the following summer at Collioure where he showed the younger artist how to obtain the greatest luminosity by leaving patches of the canvas bare white to represent the sun's rays. This was Derain's most productive period and he produced thirty oils, twenty drawings and fifty sketches whilst at Collioure.

What these men had in common was the use of intense violent colours combined with fluidly defined forms in their compositions. Their identity as a group and subsequent notoriety was established at the 1905 Salon d'Automne when, characteristically, a critic singled out a meek white torso in the middle of the room full of these blazingly vivid paintings, and called it *"Donatello chez les fauves"* The name "Fauve" (or wild beast) stuck. The Fauve room was referred to as "the cage" and "the chosen room of pictorial aberration and tonal madness".

Fauvism was one of the final and most violent assaults on official art. Vlaminck claimed to have instigated the movement. "It is my rejection of academic teaching and regimentation, my blues, my red, my yellows, my pure colours without tonal admixtures." Colour was used in an arbitrary way to express power. The movement however was short-lived; its most productive period was from 1906 to 1909. After the Salon des Indépendants and the Cézanne retrospective exhibition of 1907, Derain voiced his disillusion with the practice of colour shock tactics for its own sake. Vlaminck also said: "I suffered for not being able to hit harder, for having arrived at the maximum intensity." The importance of Matisse was growing. He had developed faster than any of them and had learnt to structure colour, rather than use it as an end in itself. It had to interact with line and pattern to acquire any real meaning. As a former pupil of Gustave Moreau, he had never forgotten the importance the Symbolists attached to line and pattern. Gauguin too was moving in step with these ideas and Matisse later studied the iconology of his Breton pictures. He also combined the bold architectural planes of Cézanne with the frankness of Manet's *Olympia* and Degas's *Woman at her Toilet* to produce the starkly realistic *Carmelina* which depicts a nude model sitting on a table gazing fearlessly out at the viewer in full frontal splendour. Matisse looked for "chromatic equivalences" from local colour and said, "when I place a green, this does not mean grass; when I place a blue this does not mean sky... I use red for a green marble table. Elsewhere,

Self portrait, 1900
drawing by Henri Matisse

I need a black spot to create the idea of the sun's rays sparkling on the sea." The transposition of the colour of paint on the palette to that conjured up out of the painter's mind was the prerogative Matisse established before twentieth-century art chased it through to total abstraction.

With the demise of Fauvism in 1908, Matisse produced linear designs that develop organically like a plant or a river. He studied Byzantine mosaics, Persian and Eastern painting, Talavera pottery and textiles in order to refine his use of colour for abstract purposes, and added to this a bold cursive style as seen in *The Dance* (1909-10) where five nude figures link up in a rhythmic circle.

Derain in the same year, 1908 sold many of his Fauve pictures to Vollard and destroyed the rest. He also exchanged Matisse for Picasso as mentor. Dufy turned his calligraphic talent to textile design while Van Dongen used brash colours to spotlight the seductive and jaded faces of vampish "mondaines".

Georges Rouault, never a Fauve in the strict sense, continued his series of harlequin and circus subjects, etched religious scenes (*Passion* and *Miserere*) and painted grotesque superheroes like the warmonger, Le Père Ubu, who were haunting reminders of the devastated spirits of the Great War years.

By 1908, there was nothing left to be learned from Impressionism. The progress of Picasso, who was absorbing influences and ideas at a furious rate, taking what he needed before discarding them, astounded everyone. His paintings in Paris between 1900 and 1903 were influenced in subject matter (the harlequin and circus figures) by Degas and Lautrec. After his romantic melancholy Blue Period in Barcelona from 1903 to 1905 he returned to Paris to work alongside Braque to develop Cubism. This was a working out in portraiture and still life of Cézanne's observation that "all nature is modelled on the sphere, the cone and the cylinder." Colour had been liberated, the picture surface was an autonomous whole judged on its own terms; the imagination now dictated the forms we see. Post-Impressionist art, in its collective and tangential groupings from the mid 1880s to 1907, was a gestation period prior to the birth of abstraction. All modern artists from Mondrian to Barnett Newman are indebted to the radical ideas on colour and line formulated at that time.

Bibliography
The author has consulted the following works in the writing of this book:

Post Impressionism: From Van Gogh to Gauguin *by John Rewald*
Van Gogh, Gauguin and the Post-Impressionist Circle *by Mark Roskill*
The Post Impressionists *by Frank Elgar*
Modern French Painters *by R.H. Wilenski*
Georges Seurat (Introduction) *by Roger Fry*

Georges Seurat *by John Rewald*
Gauguin *by Georges Boudaille*
Paul Gauguin, Noa-Noa, Voyage to Tahiti translated *by Jonathan Griffin*
The Drawings of Gauguin *by Ronald Pickvance*
Gauguin *by Daniel Wildenstein and Raymond Cogniat*
Vincent Van Gogh *by Meyer Schapiro*
Van Gogh *by Jacques Lassaigne*
The Letters of Van Gogh (edited) *by Mark Roskill*
Stranger on the Earth – The Life of Vincent van Gogh *by Albert J. Lubin*

Cézanne: His art, his work *by Lionello Venturi*
The Letters of Paul Cézanne (edited) *by John Rewald*
Cézanne *by Frank Elgar*
The Fauvist Painters *by Georges Duthuit*
Fauvism *by J.E. Muller*
Matisse: His art and his public *by Alfred H. Barr Jr.*
Henri Rousseau: Portrait of a Primitive *by Ronald Alley*
A Concise History of Modern Painting *by Herbert Read*